# I WAS A DOCTOR
# IN AUSCHWITZ

by

## Dr. Gisella Perl

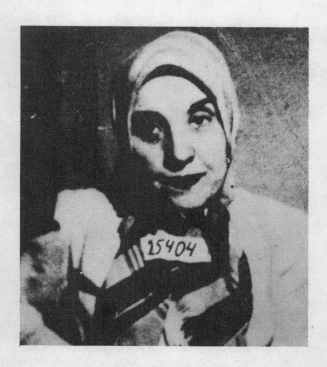

**YALE GARBER**
**Tamarac, Fl.**
**1987**

# OUT OF DEATH, A ZEST FOR LIFE

## By NADINE BROZAN

*Reprinted from The New York Times Monday, November 15, 1982*

Every time Dr. Gisella Perl enters a delivery room, she stops first to pray: "God, you owe me a life, a living baby."

That debt was incurred in Auschwitz in World War II, when the Hungarian gynecologist, who was both inmate and physician at the concentration camp, realized that to save the lives of hundreds of pregnant women, she would have to prevent them from giving birth.

Thirty-seven years and thousands of safe deliveries later, Dr. Perl, 72 years old, is recognized in Israel, where she now lives, and elsewhere by grateful women who fall to their knees and call her "Gisi Doctor." That was the name by which they knew her in the concentration camp.

In Shaare Zedek Medical Center in Jerusalem, she now donates her time to the center's gynecological clinics.

But the past is never out of mind. She calls herself the Ambassador of the Six Million and talks of the past incessantly, in private conversation and in the speeches she gives to raise funds for the medical center.

"The greatest crime in Auschwitz was to be pregnant," she said in an interview the other day, recalling the edicts of Josef Mengele. The so-called doctor of death of Auschwitz performed savage medical experiments on prisoners, in particular, women, the physically handicapped and twins, and was in charge of deciding who would go to the gas chambers.

### The Loss of Two Lives

"Dr. Mengele told me that it was my duty to report every pregnant women to him," Dr. Perl said. "He said that they would go to another camp for better nutrition, even for milk. So women began to run directly to him, telling him, 'I am pregnant.' I learned that they were all taken to the research block to be used as guinea pigs, and then two lives would be thrown into the crematorium. I decided that never again would there be a pregnant woman in Auschwitz."

She interrupted the pregnancies, she said, "in the night, on a dirty floor, using only my dirty hands."

"Hundreds of times I had premature deliveries," she said. "No one will ever know what it meant to me to destroy those babies, but if I had not done it, both mother and child would have been cruelly murdered."

But all of medicine was her province in the camp. As one of five doctors and four nurses chosen by Dr. Mengele to operate a hospital ward that had no beds, no bandages, no drugs and no instruments, she tended to every disease wrought by torture, starvation, filth, lice and rats, to every bone broken or head cracked open by beating. She performed surgery, without anesthesia, on women whose breasts had been lacerated by whips and become infected.

Dr. Perl had only one palliative: the spoken word. "I treated patients with my voice, telling them beautiful stories, telling them that one day we would have birthdays again, that one day we would sing again. I didn't know when it was Rosh ha-Shanah, but I had a sense of it when the weather turned cool. So I made a party with the bread, margarine and dirty pieces of sausage we received for meals. I said tonight will be the New Year, tomorrow a better year will come."

Dr. Perl was seized by the Gestapo along with her parents and husband in March 1944 and taken by cattle car from her hometown of Sighet (in what is now Rumania) to Auschwitz, in Poland. She was never to see them again, but the memory of her father, Maurice Perl, being led away, clutching a prayer book, remains vivid.

The prayer book symbolized a vow she had made years earlier. At age 16, Gisella Perl had graduated first in her secondary-school class, the only woman and the only Jew. She asked her father to send her to medical school, but he refused at first, saying as she remembers it, "'I do not want my daughter to lose her faith and break away from Judaism.'"

## 'A Good, True Jew'

Several months later, she approached him again, this time with a prayer book he had given her, and said, "I swear on this book that wherever life will take me, under whatever circumstances, I shall always remain a good, true Jew."

Maurice Perl relented, and she enrolled in medical school. Years later, on the day she was paid a fee by her first patient, she bought another prayer book and had engraved on it her father's name. Again she declared to him, "I swear on this prayer book that wherever life shall take me I will remain an observant Jew."

Her father carried that book into the crematorium in Auschwitz.

In January 1945, as Russian forces approached, the Germans hastily shut down gas chambers and evacuated the camps. Dr. Perl was moved to a camp near Hamburg, then, two months later, to Bergen-Belsen, a camp in Germany that she described in a book she wrote after the war as "the supreme fulfillment of German sadism and bestiality." At the precise moment that British troops were moving in to liberate Bergen-Belsen, Dr. Perl was delivering a baby, the first free child born there.

She remained in the camp until the fall, when she wandered throughout Germany by foot searching for her family. After 19 days, she learned that her husband had been beaten to death just before the liberation and her teenage son, who had been taken from her when she was deported, had died in a gas chamber. It was only then that she succumbed to grief and tried to poison herself. Subsequently she was taken to a convent in France to recuperate.

In March 1947 she came to this country to speak to doctors and other professionals. "I went from one town to another, as an ambassador of the six million," she said, "One day Eleanor Roosevelt came to the dais and invited me to lunch. I remember saying, 'Oh, Mrs. President, I cannot come because I am kosher.' She said, 'You will have a kosher lunch.'"

Mrs. Roosevelt told her, "'Stop torturing yourself; become a doctor again,'" she recalled. "I didn't want to be a doctor; I just wanted to be a witness."

As a result of that meeting, Representative Sol Bloom, Democrat of New York, intorduced the bill that granted her citizenship, and in 1951 she opened an office in Manhattan, with what she calls "Sol Bloom furniture."

"I was the poorest doctor on Park Avenue, but I had the greatest practice; all of Auschwitz and Bergen-Belsen were my patients," she said. She also joined the staff of Mount Sinai Hospital and worked for Dr. Alan F. Guttmacher, the family-planning pioneer who was chairman of obstetrics and gynecology. She delivered 3,000 babies in New York and became an expert in treating infertility.

Three years ago, she decided to move to Israel to fulfill another old vow. "After four days in the cattle car that took us to Auschwitz, suddenly the S.S. officers opened the door, and prisoners in striped pajamas threw us out," she recalled. "My father and husband both embraced me, saying, 'Swear we will never go back, we will meet someday in Jerusalem.'"

Now she lives in Herzliya with her daughter, Gabriella Krauss Blattmann, who was hidden during the war with a non-Jewish family, and has a 32-year-old grandson.

Today, even as she expresses fear of a resurgence of anti-Semitism, she says: "It is worthwhile to live. God rewarded me. He rewards me even more now."

## ACKNOWLEDGMENT

I am deeply indebted to Mr. Michael Koch
for his generous help in the preparation
of the manuscript.

To the Memory

of

**My Husband and My Son**

# SHAARE ZEDEK'S INTERNATIONAL FAMILY OF FRIENDS

## OFFICES

**U.S.A.**
American Committee for Shaare Zedek
Hospital in Jerusalem Inc.

**NATIONAL OFFICE**
49 West 45th Street
New York, N.Y. 10036
Tel: (212) 354-8801

**MID-ATLANTIC REGION**
220 South 16th Street, Suite 401
Philadelphia, PA 19102
Tel: (215) 735-3306

**SOUTHEAST REGION**
605 Lincoln Road, Suite 211
Miami Beach, Fla. 33139
Tel: (305) 531-8329

**MID-CENTRAL & MIDWEST REGIONS**
3570 Warrensville Center Rd.
Shaker Heights, Ohio 44122
Tel: (216) 283-9222

**WESTERN REGION**
292 South La Cienega Blvd., Suite 216
Beverly Hills CA 90211
Tel: (213) 659-6800

**SAN FRANCISCO COMMITTEE**
354 El Dorado Drive
Daly City, CA 94015
Tel: (415) 755-1300

**SEATTLE COMMITTEE**
10323 S.E. 13th Place
Bellevue, Washington, 98004
Tel: (206) 454-4626

**DETROIT COMMITTEE**
24651 Sussex
Oak Park, Mich. 48237
Tel: (313) 968-3288

**CANADA**
Canadian Shaare Zedek
Hospital Foundation

**NATIONAL OFFICE**
3089 Bathurst St., #205
Toronto, Ontario M6A 2A4
Tel: (416) 781-3584

5180 Queen Mary, Suite 350
Montreal, Quebec H3W 3E7
Tel: (514) 486-7301

**SOUTH AFRICA**
S.A. Friends of Shaare Zedek Hospital
P.O. Box 27738
Yeoville, Johannesburg
Tel: 648-9409

**UNITED KINGDOM**
British Council of the Shaare Zedek
Medical Centre
College House, New College Parade
Finchley Road
London NW3 5EP
Tel: 01-586-2948/9

## COMMITTEES

**AUSTRALIA**
Australian Friends of Shaare Zedek Hospital
Mr. J. Feiglin
7 Labassa Grove
Caulfield 3161, Melbourne
Tel: 527-1207

**EUROPE**
Denmark, Finland, Gibralter,
Holland, Italy, Norway, Sweden
Mr. Bernard Zimmer
Hon. European Chairman
943 Finchley Road
London NW11 7PE
Tel: (01) 458-1336

**BELGIUM**
Mme. Sara Brachfeld
7 Colmasstraat
Deurne Zuid
2000 Antwerp

**DENMARK**
Mr. B. Zimmer
Bulowsvej 28
1870 Copenhagen V

**FRANCE**
Mr. Henri Glasberg
64 rue Lafayette
75009 Paris

**GERMANY**
Herr Simon Preisler
Leibigstrasse 9
D. 6000 Frankfurt/Main

**HOLLAND**
Mevr. Lotte Bio
Minervalaan 41 hs
Amsterdam

**SWITZERLAND**
Frau Berti Schwartz
20 Todistrasse
8002 Zurich

**SOUTH AMERICA**
VENEZUELA
Presidenta Sra Henny Brener
Edificio Baronet, Apto. 15A
Parque Residential, Anauco
Av. Los Proceres
San Bernardino
Caracas 1011

Committees are active in
ARGENTINA & MEXICO
For Brazil contct B. Zimmer
Hon. European Chairman in London.

# CONTENTS

Foreword ................................................... 11
Dr. Kapezius ............................................. 13
"I Want to Go with Them..." .......................... 20
Arrival at Auschwitz ................................... 25
Auschwitz—and A Day within its Borders ............. 30
Dinner at Auschwitz .................................... 37
The "Beauty Parlor" .................................... 41
Auschwitz Treasure-Trove. Julika Farkas ............. 47
Charlotte Junger ........................................ 52
The Value of a Piece of String... ...................... 55
Irma Greze .............................................. 60
"Concert" in Auschwitz ................................ 65
Margarine ............................................... 68
Block VII: The Latrine .................................. 72
Childbirth in Camp C ................................... 79
The Hospital Staff ...................................... 86
The Story of the Fatal Handkerchief ................... 95
One Woman's Death ....................................102
The Bag of Diamonds ...................................109
The Life-Saving Embryo ................................113
The Story of Jeanette ...................................120
Liquidation of Camp C .................................124
Farewell to Auschwitz ..................................127
Trip to Hamburg ........................................138
Hamburg—Dege Werke ................................146
Belsen Bergen ...........................................157
General Gleen Hughes ..................................161
Abbé Brand .............................................166

# ACKNOWLEDGEMENTS

The project of reprinting Dr. Perl's book has been a labor of love for both myself and Nat "Duby" Dubinsky.

It was our privilege to meet Dr. Perl while attending a Board of Directors meeting of the Shaare Zedek Medical Center in Jerusalem, where she still works in the gynocological clinic.

When we learned that her book was out of print, we immediately set about to have it reprinted. Her story must not be forgotten.

Grateful acknowledgement is made to the following for their help and assistance:

Yale Garber

Typographic Directions Corp.
Len Horn
Barbara Dubrinsky
Abraham David
Walter Dornfest
Milton Wildman
Jerry Leibowitz
Martin Breit
Ruth Cohen
Jerrold F. and Jane Goodman
Mark and Selma Denburg
Louis and Etta Aronson
Beulah Feldman

Irwin and Bashie Selevan
Mark and Sherry Witenstein
Morris Talansky
Saul Zabel
Fran Gerber
David Smith
Steven Lescht
Ed Ouellette
Charles Newman
Murray Miller
Kurt Walter
Alice Marks
Harry Fishbein

10

# FOREWORD

Heinrich Heine, the great German poet, predicted a hundred years ago the inevitable "renaissance" of the spirit of destruction, inherent in the German soul.

"Christianity has, to a certain point, soothed the brutal martial spirit of the Germans," he said, "but that spirit is not destroyed. When the Cross, the talisman that kept it in chains, shall be broken, then the ferocity of ancient combatants shall revive and the frenzied exaltation of which Nordic poets still sing will again take possession of the Germans. Then, and this way is unfortunately sure to come, the ancient deities of war will rise from their mystic tombs, wipe the dust of centuries out of their eyes and, lifting their gigantic hammers, they will demolish the Gothic Cathedrals..."

Yes, Heine was right. The ancient, sadistic German rose from his grave, donned an S.S. uniform and, lifting his infernal hooked cross in mockery of the Cross of Christ, went forth to destroy, burn, plunder, torture and murder. Hitler, this degenerate Faust, and his henchmen turned the German people into a willing instrument of conquest and massacre.

We shall never be able to understand how a people which produced Kant, Goethe, Beethoven, Bach, Dürer and many other incomparable geniuses could sink so deep in the morass of depravity, crime and the enjoyment of torture that every human being who watched them felt ashamed of belonging to the same species.

I offer this book as a monument commemorating the events of the years 1940-1945, commemorating Nazi bestiality, Nazi sadism, Nazi inhumanity and the death of their six million innocent Jewish victims. Every individual story, every picture, every description is but a stone in that monument which will stand forever to remind the world of this shameful phase of history and to ask of it vigilance, lest the events of these years be repeated.

"L'Allegemagne Éternelle," which boasts of the ruthless cruelty of its people, shows its real face on the pages of this book. You, who have spent your lives under the protection of the Statue of Liberty, stop before this monument and read its inscriptions. Read them, engrave them in your souls and carry them with you as a memento! The dead are speaking to you here. The dead, who do not ask you to avenge them but only to remember them and to be watchful that no more innocent victims of German inhumanity ever swell their ranks...

G. P., July, 1946.

# DR. KAPEZIUS

December 1943, Maramaros Sziget, Transylvania. —After years of fear, sorrow and an unrelenting fight against hopelessness and resignation, the hunters had at last become the hunted. In ever-increasing numbers the Nazi "conquerors" came streaming through our town, cold, hungry and bewildered, thrown back towards the West by the irresistible impact of the Russian counter-offensive. As we saw their emaciated bodies, their frozen hands and rag-clad feet, there was no more compassion in our hearts than there was in the heart of the Maramaros mountains, whose snow-capped peaks remained untouched by the changing tides of history. To every Jewish mother, wife and sister, the German soldier was the symbol of all evil. We hated him with a fierce and unquenchable hatred. It was he who was responsible for the fate of our men, drafted into slave labor batallions and driven into the Russian winter, half starved, in rags, unarmed, to destroy land-mines and clear the way for the German armies. Those who were not killed by the explosions died of exposure, starvation or the cruel beatings administered as a reward for their servitude. But now, with the retreating armies, some of the survivors returned, almost unrecognizable, with long beards, and faces aged with suffering. But they were alive and—we thought—safe.

I was doing the work of three in those days, replacing several gynecologists who had gone with the labor battalions. I helped young mothers bring their babies into the world, easing their pains by telling them long, optimistic stories about a peaceful, secure future in which there would be no more Nazis to endanger their lives and the lives of their children. I was untiring and full of hope, revived by the winds of liberation blowing from the East and from the West.

One afternoon, a quiet, well-mannered German gentleman came to see me at my office.

"I am Dr. Kapezius," he introduced himself, "medical propagandist of the *I.G. Farbenindustie.* I have come to bring you some of our newest preparations, but—to be perfectly candid—this is only an excuse. I am not interested in the *I.G. Farben* of today. They are an integral part of the Nazi system, and although I still represent them, I do not care whether I sell their products or not. I am here because I know that you and your husband spent much time in Berlin during the Weimar Republic, and I want to talk about Germany as it was in those days and as it will be again after Nazism is defeated. Please, try to trust me…Believe me, there are many people in Germany who, like me, live only for the day of liberation…"

Trust him I couldn't. At least not at first. But admonishing myself that one shouldn't condemn a nation for the crimes of some of its sons, even if they were the majority, I invited him to my house to meet my husband and my son.

The long evening we spent together stands out in my

memory like a colorful painting against a background of black. We lived in a beautiful house which had belonged to Cornelia Priel, the great Hungarian artist of French origin. Within the walls of my green salon, surrounded by the love and admiration of my husband and my son, I felt happy and secure. It was there that every evening I gathered the strength and will to continue my work which was becoming increasingly difficult. On the night of Dr. Kapezius' visit, we talked about music and literature, about the artistic and scientific achievements of pre-Hitler Germany. As the evening wore on, our confidence in Dr. Kapezius' sincere love for freedom and his hatred for the Nazis grew until our dreams of post-war Europe became bolder and bolder. He shared all our views and helped spin out the beautiful pattern we drew before his eyes. When I recited poems by Heine and Lessing, his eyes filled with tears, and when my son played for him Hubay's "Violinist from Cremona," his praise and enthusiasm knew no bounds. Overwhelmingly thankful for the wonderful evening he had spent in what he called a "shrine of culture in Eastern Europe," he shook my hand warmly, admiring my unusual wristwatch, and left, reiterating that the day of freedom was near. "Keep up your courage," were his last words to us.

Five months later I was to see him again, in the second month of my stay at Auschwitz, clad in an S.S. *Haupsturm-fuehrer* uniform. He was the Commander of the camp.

"Jewish physicians step out of the lines!" Dr. Mengerle, chief physician of the camp ordered. "We are going to establish a hospital."

Along with a few others I stepped forward and came face to face with Dr. Kapezius, standing beside the chief physician. I had just recovered from an unsuccessful attempt at suicide. My head was shaved and the dirty rags which covered my body did not hide my pitifully weakened condition. For one second, I could not believe my eyes. In a flash I saw my home, my son holding the violin under his chin, my husband and our guest listening to him with rapt attention. The scene revolved in front of my eyes while his face smiled mirthlessly, then darkness settled over everything. When I came to, I was lying on the floor of my block and was ordered to report to Dr. Kapezius immediately.

He looked me over from head to foot—and smiled again. When he spoke, his voice was cold and jeering and my loathing was so strong that at first I could scarcely understand his words. His voice, however, succeeded soon in reaching my consciousness. "You are going to be the camp gynecologist..." he barked. "Don't worry about instruments...you won't have any. Your medical kit belongs to me now, and also that unusual wristwatch I admired...I also have your papers, but you won't need those...You can go." I never saw him again.

But this was much later. In January and February of 1944, we were still in our home, cold, undernourished, overworked, but full of hope. There was an almost unbearable tension in the air, the little town held his breath, waiting for the break-through in the Carpathians which would save us from the inevitable brown death.

The break-through, when it came, came too late. On March 19, 1944, a sunny, Spring Sunday, the Germans overran Hungary and our fate was sealed. Quickly, quickly, so as to squeeze their whole beastly program into a short time they began bombarding us with order after order.

First we had to sew on the yellow Star of David…then came the curfew…travel was prohibited…homes were searched…people interned…stores, business requisitioned…an endless succession of sudden alarms. Then there came an order forbidding us to leave our houses for three days. We cowered in our apartments, sick with fear, waiting for the next blow. Official burglary. Police broke into house after house, demanding gold, silver, jewels, valuables, money. They opened cupboards, drawers, closets, took everything they fancied, unmindful of our presence as though we were already dead.

And when we had been deprived of all our possessions, we were driven into the Ghetto carrying on our backs small bundles containing bare necessities. At the end of the town there were a few narrow, dirty, muddy streets lined by dilapidated shacks. Eight to ten people had to share one room. Living was reduced to its lowest level. Still, it was home. We could still watch the sun go down over our mountains and we could still hope in our hearts that our liberators would soon come down the mountain slopes. We had our friends and relatives around us, and their love brightened the fear which filled our souls.

The Ghetto served only one purpose. It made it easier for our persecutors to rob us of our last meager possessions. They came morning and night, without giving us any respite, searched our rooms, our clothes, and nothing and no one was immune to their relentless quest. It was on a Saturday—I remember—that we learned we would be searched for hidden jewels once more. This time it was the Gestapo, not the local authorities who performed the operation. When they had gone through everything without finding any valuables, I had to stand by and watch while they seized one woman after another and with dirty fingers searched the depths of her body for treasures.

Then, one day, the head of the Gestapo ordered me to establish a hospital and a maternity ward in the Ghetto. Winged with happiness, I ran from house to house, begging for a spare bed, a sheet, a towel, some cotton, wool, a pillow, whatever they could do without, and in a few days a little apartment had been transformed into a clean, white almost comfortable hospital. It was then that I had my first encounter with German perversity. The establishing of the hospital gave us a feeling of security. " Why should they tell us to organize a hospital," we said to one another, "if they intend to deport us? Maybe we won't be deported after all…Maybe they'll keep us here, in the Ghetto, until the war is over. Maybe they need their trains for the transportation of their retreating armies and the Russian counteroffensive may well save our lives."

After I had performed my first delivery at the new maternity hospital—a complicated instrument delivery— the head of the Gestapo arrived with a few diapers as a present for the newborn child. He congratulated me on my skill, admired the work I had done in creating the hospital and showed a friendly interest in everything I told him. The very next day the order for deportation came from Berlin, and the Gestapo chief came personally to throw the young mother and her day-old child into the cattle car.

When we learned of the deportation order, my husband, who was president of the Jewish Council of the Ghetto and as such responsible for carrying out all orders, went to see the Gestapo chief and begged him, as a favor, to execute the whole Ghetto then and there. He and his family would be the first to go to their death, he said. The answer was a gust of laughter and a beating that sent him flying down the steps of headquarters. We picked him up, unconscious, and carried him back to our room. Next day, at dawn, we had to leave the Ghetto after two weeks of miserable life there. First we were sent to the Temple where we were again searched, deprived of our small bundles, and our few papers and photographs were destroyed. Then, like cattle, we were driven to the station and put into cattle cars, eighty to one hundred persons crowded into each car. In vain dread we look to the mountains, the town, the people for help. Only death was to deliver us from our suffering.

# "I WANT TO GO WITH THEM..."

Today—when everything seems so helpless in this chaotic world of ours, when, after all the bloodshed, all the suffering of the past years, peace and security are still unknown blessings everywhere—people like me, who have gone through hell, often ask themselves the question: Where will this end? Will goodness, love, justice never again reign on this earth? Will hate and evil always wield the scepter?

My questions remain unanswered, but whenever I ask them I remember a little story which proves to me that responsibility for the world we live in lies not with man but rather with his education. I remember a young girl named Elizabeth and my faith in the inherent nobility of man, which can be roused in response to kindness, is revived.

It happened on a cold, windy December night, in the valley of the snow-capped Carpathians. The long, hard ringing of the doorbell broke the silence of the night. Then the voice of a nurse: "They have brought in a woman, Doctor. She is bleeding. Will you come?"

A few minutes later I was in the operating room. A young girl, about sixteen years old, lay on the operating table, covered with blood, a victim of rape. Soon the stitches were put in, the wound was cleaned and the girl rested silently on the white hospital bed. I did not ask her any questions. It was night; she had to sleep; there would be time enough tomorrow.

Elizabeth stayed at the hospital for a week, and during that week she told me all about her sad little life. She was an orphan, Protestant, Hungarian. She was living with some relatives where toil and beatings were her daily fare. Even her nights were not her own; they were disturbed by the loud, drunken antics of the master of the house. It was on such a night, when drunk, crazy with alcoholic passion, he raped the little girl who was not strong enough to resist his brutality.

"Don't make me go back there, Doctor..." she repeated day after day, "I'd rather die than go back."

She stayed with me. I sent her to school to learn cooking and she became my housekeeper. My son was like a brother to her. They studied together Latin and French and literature, they recited poetry together, read history and geography; and while helping me to put away jams and jellies for the winter, Elizabeth whistled Beethoven and Mozart melodies which my son played to her on his violin. She was treated like a daughter, called my parents "grandma" and "grandpa," and she and my son planned many a childish trick, many a sweet surprise together. She shared our pleasures and worries, our dreams and desires and our sorrows.

After a while she began accompanying me to my patients and her friendship with my son was so strong that it was she to whom he confessed his little secrets. She took part in our strictly Jewish life—but she remained a Protestant. I insisted on that. I bought her a Bible and a Psalm book, and sent her to the Minister every Sunday; and when the bells of the old Protestant church rang for the services, I never failed to make her attend them. She had to fast on Good Friday; and on Christmas she always had her lovely, warmly shining Christmas tree. But she also fasted on the Jewish Holy Days; and when we lighted the Hanukka candles of the ancient Maccabees, she and my son sang the ancient songs together, in perfect harmony.

That sad December night, when, covered with blood, she lay on my operating table left in her heart a deep respect for me—a respect that was even stronger than love.

Years went by. Elizabeth became an attractive young woman. According to an old custom, we began to prepare her trousseau. And then, on a memorable day, Horror made its appearance in our house.

Brutal policemen and Gestapo men broke into our house, opened the closets and wardrobes, stole, destroyed what they could, and with filthy curses urged us to get ready. One heavy hand hit my white-haired father, a young German hero slapped my husband and one of the policemen pushed me impatiently towards the door. Over all the chaotic noise Elizabeth's voice sounded sharp and threatening like a foghorn:

"Leave Grandfather alone. Don't you dare touch the Doctor. You are not Hungarians, you are not even human! Gangsters! Murderers! These people are good Hungarians, decent human beings! Take your hands off them, you soulless brigands!"

Desperately, without a thought for her own danger,

she held out her two weak arms and tried to put her own young body between us and our persecutors.

A high fence separated the Ghetto from the world of death and violence outside; and we cowered behind it, frightened and desperate, wondering how long the safety of that fence would protect us. Day after day Elizabeth appeared at the gate with a parcel of food for us. She grew thinner and thinner and it was apparent that she herself went without food to be able to provide for us.

Then came the last afternoon we were to spend in our little city. We were already in the cattle cars and guards were nailing the doors shut upon us, when between the bars a well-known hand reached out for us, Elizabeth's hand. She brought us milk and bread for the trip; but when she saw me standing there, pressed in among my companions in misery, she lost her head completely. Crying, screaming, she began to beat her fists against the strong iron doors as if she hoped to break them down by the strength of her despair. "I want to go with them!" she cried... "Let me go with them..."

The guards got hold of her and dragged her away from the train, beating her, kicking her, to silence her hopeless screams. The train pulled out, the bell tower of the Protestant high school and the church disappeared in the distance, but the heartbroken cries of little Elizabeth followed me all the way to Auschwitz and will forever follow me wherever I go. "I am going with you...Let me go with them..."

Yes, the responsibility for the world to come lies with the educators. If we wanted it, if we really and honestly attempted to build a better world, the good in mankind would prevail and the Elizabeths would not constitute rare and memorable exceptions.

# ARRIVAL AT AUSCHWITZ

For eight days we travelled, day and night, toward an unknown goal. The police who accompanied us to the frontier spoke of a big, common Ghetto where we would be put to work. But when we saw, through the small opening of our sealed car, that the S.S. (Storm Troopers) took over our train at the frontier, we knew there was no hope for us. From then on we received no food, no water. The small children cried with hunger and cold, the old people moaned for help, some went insane, others gave life to their babies there on the dirty floor, some died and their bodies travelled on with us...Once in a while our jailers would enter the car in a renewed search for valuables, or only to beat us and silence plaintive voices with brutal threats.

Then we arrived. We strained our tired, weakened eyes to read the name of the station: AUSCHWITZ. When the S.S. guards unsealed the door of our car and ordered us to get out, I ran to my parents, embraced them and begged them to forgive me if I had ever caused them any heartaches. "You were always the best child any parents could have," they comforted me. My sisters and brothers embraced me silently. My husband drew me close. "Take

25

care of yourself ... " he whispered, "take care of your warm, generous heart ... " My son just looked at me, with his big, blue eyes. "Mother ... " they said. "Mother ... "

No one who came out alive of a German extermination camp can ever forget the picture that greeted us at Auschwitz. Like big, black clouds, the smoke of the crematory hung over the camp. Sharp red tongues of flame licked the sky, and the air was full of the nauseating smell of burning flesh. A detachment of S.S. men with guns, whips, and clubs in their hands attacked us, separating the men from their wives, parents from their children, the old from the young. Those who resisted or were too weak to move fast were beaten, kicked, and dragged away. In a few minutes we were standing in separate groups, almost unconscious with pain, fear, exhaustion, and the unbearable shock of losing our beloved ones.

Now, with a handful of S.S. officers, the camp physician took over the direction of this infernal game. With a flick of his hand he sent some of us to the left, some to the right. It took some time before I understood what this meant. Of every trainload of prisoners, ten to twelve thousand at a time, he selected about three thousand inmates for his camp. The others, those who went "left," were taken to the crematory to die a horrible death in the constantly burning fire. They were loaded into Red Cross trucks, in a weird mockery of all human decency, and carted away; and all we ever saw of them again were their clothes in the storeroom of the camp.

Later I learned all about this bestial procedure. They were taken into small wooden houses, undressed, given a towel and a piece of soap and told to stand under the shower. They were trembling with expectation, yearning for the drops of water which would cleanse their soiled, exhausted bodies after the long days of travelling, and which would quench the thirst of their dry, hot throats. But instead of water a heavy, choking gas came out of the jets. Within seven or eight minutes some of them were asphyxiated, others only became unconscious and were tossed into the flames alive. The screams, the gurgling, choking sounds coming out of those wooden houses will forever ring in my ears.

The children, little blond or dark-haired children coming from every part of Europe, did not go with their mothers into the gas-chambers. They were taken away, crying and screaming, with wild terror in their eyes, to be undressed, thrown into the waiting graves, drenched with some inflammable material and burned alive. Hundreds of thousands of little children, the beautiful and the plain ones, the rich and the poor, the well-mannered and the naughty, the healthy and the sick, blue-eyed blond Polish children, dark-haired little Hungarians, round-faced Dutch babies, solemn little French boys and girls, all died to satisfy the sadistic instincts of these perverts.

We, who by mere chance were sent to the "right," formed a column and set out towards the camp. The roadside was lined up with rotting corpses showing the fate of those who fell out of line. We arrived before a large wooden building and were told to enter.

But suddenly the column disintegrated, the unbearable tension exploded and the terror, the pain, the sorrow, and the loneliness turned women into screaming, panicky, and hysterical creatures. They refused to enter the build-

ing which had the sign *Disinfection* painted on it in big letters. Bullets flew, whips cracked and clubs fell with a dull
sound, leaving broken bones and open skulls in their wake
— but the pandemonium would not subside.

"Where is a doctor?" yelled one of the S.S. men. I
stepped forward. He stood me on a table and I was given
the first order of my camp-life.

"Tell these animals to keep quiet or I'll have them
all shot!"

"Listen to me ..." I called to them. "Do not be afraid!
This is only a disinfection center, nothing will happen to
you here. Afterwards we'll be put to work, we'll all remain
together, friends, sisters in our common fate. I am your
doctor ... I'll stay with you, always, to take care of you, to
protect you ... Please, calm down ..."

My words had their effect. The women believed me,
they fell silent and entered the building, one after another.
Under the supervision of S.S. men and women, other prisoners carried out the program of disinfection. We were
undressed there before the laughing S.S. guards who
showed their appreciation for some of the beautiful bodies
by slashing them with whips. Everything that could have
reminded us of our past life was taken away from us.

When we came out of the building we did not know
each other any more. Instead of the exhausted, tortured,
but still self-respecting women who entered through
its door, we were a heart-rending lot of crying clowns,
a ghastly carnival procession marching toward the last
festival: death ...

I was beyond caring. After my encouraging speech to
the hysterical women I had swallowed the forty centigrams

of morphine which I had hidden in a small bottle. I felt an ironical superiority as I held out my head to the scissors and smiled under the ice-cold shower...My feet were winged by the effect of morphine as I entered the doors of Auschwitz, certain that I was going toward the supreme happiness of oblivion.

# AUSCHWITZ—AND A DAY WITHIN ITS BORDERS

Auschwitz, which housed the largest Nazi extermination camp, lies in Upper Silesia, about twenty-five miles from Kattowitz. As if Nature had created it for just this purpose, even the soil itself is dead; no tree, no flower relieves its grey monotony.

To our life there, which was already beyond endurance, the mud and heavy clay which stuck to our wooden shoes added an almost insurmountable difficulty. There was no water, except for the rain which swept cold and hard over the flatness of the entire reservation, seeping into the barracks and forming icy rivulets on the thin, wooden walls of our last refuge. The only animals we ever saw were crows, rats and lice, which shared our miserable life by stealing the crumbs out of our mouths, building their nests in our cages and crawling over our sleeping bodies at night.

The approximately forty square miles of Auschwitz were divided into smaller camps marked by different letters of the alphabet. These camps were separated from one another by barbed-wire fences with high-voltage electric current running through them. A similar electric wire fence surrounded the entire reservation. It often happened that women who could no longer stand the inhuman tortures threw themselves on these wires, hoping to end their lives quickly and so-to-say, easily. But fate was not so merciful. The current was not strong enough to kill, and they remained hanging on the fence, sometimes for days, suffering unimaginable torture until they either died from exposure or were shot to death by a guard.

Each camp consisted of endless rows of blocks—dirty, rat-infested wooden barracks—housing about twelve-hundred persons each. Along the inner walls of the barracks, there were three rows of wooden shelves, one above the other, and these shelves were our bedrooms, living-rooms, dining-rooms and studies, all in one. They were divided by vertical planks at regular intervals. Each of these cage-like contraptions served as sleeping-room for thirty to thirty-six persons. Once in a while the shelves would collapse under the weight of the sleepers and the inmates fell on one another in a bloody medley resulting in broken bones, bleeding wounds, loud wailings, and more often than not, a whipping by the "Blockova," the block superintendent.

A few "washrooms" were scattered over the camp, with one single faucet in each and a big sign above it: "Attention! Polluted water! Not for drinking!" But what did we care! We drank it all the same, we had to drink to cool our burning tongues and stomachs which were constantly on fire from the saltpeter mixed in our food. There was one latrine for thirty to thirty-two thousand women, and we were permitted to use it only at certain hours of the day. We stood in line to get into this tiny building, knee-deep in human excrement. As we all suffered from dysentery, we could rarely wait until our turn came, and soiled our ragged clothes, which never came off our bodies, thus adding to the horror of our existence by the terrible smell which surrounded us like a cloud. The latrine consisted of a deep ditch with planks thrown across it at certain intervals. We squatted on these planks like birds perched on a telegraph wire, so close together that we could not help soiling one another.

No one who had to live without the small comforts of even the poorest kind of life can imagine what it is to have to do, for instance, without paper. There was, of course, no toilet paper in the latrine and we had no way of obtaining paper except when somebody stole some from the storerooms around the crematories. We got into the habit of tearing tiny squares of material off our shirts, drying our eyes with them first, then using them to clean our rectum. However careful we were, the shirts got shorter and shorter until there was nothing left but the shoulder straps and a narrow strip around our chests. And then somebody denounced our practices and the S.S. decided to hold a shirt inspection.

One morning, at *Zählappell* (roll call), we had to lift our skirts and hold them up while laughing S.S. men walked through our lines whipping our naked bodies and selecting many among us to die in the flames as a punishment for having damaged "camp property".

Life in Auschwitz began at four o'clock in the morning when we had to crawl forth from our holes to stand for roll call in the narrow streets separating one block from another. We stood in rows of five, at arm's length from one another, soundless and motionless for four, five, or six hours at a time, in any kind of weather, all year round. When we were ready to faint with exhaustion, our torturers arrived, fresh, gay and ready for new feasts of torture. The number had to be complete, even the dying and dead had to be brought out to stand at attention. If anyone did not.appear, she was tracked down and thrown into the flames, alive. The same punishment was meted out to those who collapsed, fainted, or cried out with pain when hit by a whip. Often, for God knows what reason, the S.S. decided to punish us, and after roll call all one-hundred-and-fifty thousand of us had to kneel down in the snow or mud, to stay there on our bruised, bleeding knees for another hour or two. How often did I see women fall out of the ranks in a dead faint, without being able to succor them, to bring them even the most primitive of comforts: a glass of water.

There was another kind of roll call, too, a practice which they called "selection." The selection was a special kind of torture invented for our benefit, during which we died and resurrected a thousand times, thrown back and forth between despair and hope, our eyes, our whole being concentrated on Dr. Mengerle's hands. Those hands had the power either to condemn us to immediate execution or to prolong our miserable life by a few days...With an easy nonchalance the young, handsome, elegant camp doctor pointed to those who looked ill or weak, whose faces he did not like or who simply fell into the radius of his gesture. Two to three hundred people at a time were then pulled out of the lines, some screaming and fighting, some resigned and dignified, some too stunned to understand what was going on, to be thrown on the ever-present black Red Cross trucks and carted off to the crematories, to be given the only kind of freedom that existed for us: death...

After the morning roll call we were permitted to crawl back into our cages to stretch out for a moment before dinner distribution began.

After "dinner" we had two hours to ourselves. The use of this short time was developed into an art. It filled our thoughts day and night and we planned every minute of it as carefully as in the past we used to plan our work, our entertainment, our studies. First we ran to the water faucet to still our burning thirst, fighting, pushing, screaming at one another, trembling that time would be up before we could obtain a few drops of the life-sustaining liquid. Sometimes we could secure enough water to rub down our bodies, but most of the time we had to content ourselves with taking off our rags and shaking the lice out of them. After the battle for water was fought, we hurried to find our friends and relatives, exchange a few words of affection, and comfort one another with the hope that the day of liberation was near...if we could only keep alive until then.

Before we had time to recover from the morning roll call, the call for afternoon roll call rang through the camp. Again we had to line up in rows of five, again we had to stand soundless and motionless at arm's length from one another, in rain, snow, wind, hail, or scorching sunshine; wondering whether selection, or beating, or kneeling on the ground would follow this horrible routine. All the time we kept our faces turned towards the sky, watching the red glow of the crematories taint the clouds, and we swallowed bitter, hopeless tears for the people whose bodies turned into the ashes which covered the ground and into the soot which blackened our upturned faces.

After the second roll call, came the distribution of supper. This meal consisted of two hundred grams of bread baked of the lowest grade of flour mixed with saw dust, and a dab of margarine or a spoonful of smelly marmalade or a slice of putrid sausage. We had to consume our fare sitting in our bunks in complete darkness as there was no light whatsoever permitted in the barracks. The building was filled with noise, complaints, screams, and desperate sobs. Some cried with physical pain, others mourned their recently murdered relatives or friends, and others, again, cried because their piece of bread had been stolen in the scramble for food. There was an unbearable tension in the air which turned the prisoners against one another and bred hostility instead of solidarity. To reach the upper bunks we had to climb over the edge of the two lower shelves and it often happened that in the darkness we stepped on one another's hands, feet or even heads. These accidents brought forth torrents of curses and cruel words and the noise would serve as a provocation for another severe beating before the day was over.

The Nazi method of completely dehumanizing us before throwing us into the fire worked beautifully. Only a very few, the strongest, the cleanest, the noblest were able to retain a semblance of human dignity; the rest were engulfed by the gurgling swamp of crime, mental deterioration and filth.

Soon after supper we were silenced by the brutal voices of the guards outside: *"Lager Ruhe!"* Silence! Huddled together, body against body in a medley of arms, legs and heads, we fell asleep on the hard planks, without pillow, without blanket, to dream of days long past, of food, water, comfort and the proximity of our loved ones…

# DINNER AT AUSCHWITZ

We had always known that hunger existed. We had read Knut Hamsum's book *"Hunger"* and suffered together with his hero, and we had read Fink's *I am hungry...* But the great writer who could describe the hunger we had to endure at Auschwitz has yet to be born.

No one who has not experienced the unbearable pain of hunger during the intervals between Auschwitz dinners has any idea as to what hunger really means.

At night, lying on the cold boards of our cage, we tried to pacify our throbbing entrails with the promise of food. Tomorrow we'll get dinner—we said to ourselves. Tomorrow they'll distribute some warm food.

In the moring, when we had to stand roll call under the clouds tinged red by the flames of the crematory, we were trembling with expectancy, hardly able to stand the slow passing of time until dinner. Standing or kneeling, in scorching heat, or driving rain or snow, we had only one thought, one desire carried by our blood-stream into every part of our body: food... We were hungry. We wanted food. Warm food...

We waited for the food with the same burning impatience, the same excited imagination with which a young girl waits for her lover. Dinner was the most important moment of the day, the only moment worth living for.

The kitchen was far away from the barracks, at the end of the camp, and that was where they prepared our luxurious dinner: the turnip soup. When the soup was done, the prisoners working in the kitchen put out the tremendous pots on the street, thirty to fifty pots in a line. Then, under constant supervision by the S.S. women, these pots were carried to the barracks to be distributed among the inmates.

The block superintendent, the Blockova, chose ten to twelve prisoners to be sent for the soup. "Dinner distribution!" she yelled, and the poor, starved skeletons took their places in their cages to wait for the life-giving liquid. Our tortured stomachs hurt more and more at the thought of food, our salivary glands worked overtime and we could already feel the smell of food in our noses long before it arrived.

Finally it arrived. It was there. The superintendent stood in the middle of the floor beside the steaming pot and distributed the horrible concoction into three-quart containers, which were to serve six prisoners each. The containers were dirty and smelly, having been used the night before for entirely different purposes, but their smell blended beautifully with the indescribable smell of the turnip soup. We didn't care. It was warm and it was food, even if there were pieces of wood, potato peeling and unrecognizable substances swimming in it.

The container went from hand to hand and we swallowed quickly, convulsively, so as to get some of it down before the next in line grabbed it from our hands. We counted each other's swallows, jealously, enviously, careful that none of us should get more than her share. Sometimes we agreed that everyone should get ten mouthfuls and waited patiently for our turn. Ten miserable mouthfuls and it was over. We were hungrier than before... If only once we could have kept the whole container to ourselves! If only once we could have eaten the whole three quarts of soup alone! How much strength, how much new hope we would have gained from having our hunger stilled, at least once.

Sometimes the can fell out of a weakened hand and the soup spilled over, leaving nothing for the sixth person whose mute tears were the most terrible punishment for the offender whose carelessness had deprived her of the miserable nourishment.

Dinner was over and the barracks were loud with the screams, the plaints of the prisoners who were begging for a little more, just a little more soup. But the pots were empty; two prisoners picked them up and carried them back to the kitchen to be filled again, tomorrow, with the same miserable amount of thin, unnourishing liquid, which would again leave us hungrier, more unhappy than before.

Quickly the strongest, most energetic among us jump down from their cages and run to the door, where they catch up with the prisoners carrying the empty pot. Screaming, pushing each other aside, fighting, they stick their arms into the pot to get another mouthful of turnips or potato peeling, which stuck to the side of the pot.

Sometimes they come face to face with the last transport of soup intended for the last of the barracks. Like wild animals they attack the carriers, unmindful of the blows and kicks showering down on them, and using their palms as spoons try to get a little more food into their unsatisfied stomachs. There must have been something in that turnip soup, I don't know what, that made us hungrier than we were before.

I always was busiest after dinner. There were bleeding heads to bandage, broken ribs to be taped, scratches to be cleaned, burn wounds to be soothed. I worked and worked, knowing only too well that it was hopeless, because tomorrow everything would begin again, even the patients would probably be the same.

Dinner distribution was over, and before we had swallowed the last mouthful we already began to wait for tomorrow, hoping that then, maybe, we would at last be able to satisfy our gnawing, desperate hunger.

And not far from us, at the other end of the camp at the S.S. kitchen, cooks dressed in white were preparing the most elaborate dishes, white bread, sweets, and real coffee with cream, for our jailers...

# THE "BEAUTY PARLOR"

Every time I pass by a beauty parlor in New York, I stop to watch the young and older women who come out of its door, freshly made up, massaged, shampooed, re-created by many clever hands to look their best for their own pleasure and for the admiring eyes of their husbands and friends. And every time I see them I remember another "beauty parlor", the one in Auschwitz...

Yes, Auschwitz had a "beauty parlor", too. But its purpose was the exact opposite of that of an American beauty parlor; its purpose was to deprive its unwilling clients of even their last remnants of beauty, freshness, and human appearance. It was one of the typical Nazi jokes, a creation of their devilish imagination, which served to humiliate their victims and make their short remaining life-span all the more horrible and distressing.

The wooden building which stood near the gas chambers had *Disinfection* written on it. Everyone who was sent "right," to become a camp inmate for a while, had to pass through that building. When we entered the first of the filthy rooms inside, we were still human beings, women, wearing our own clothes, our own shoes, our own underwear, and in our hands we still carried the bundle we had brought from home, filled with all that meant so much to us. We still had hair on our heads and most of us even had hats. Above all, we still had our identity, our individuality which made us different from the other women around us, and our pride which, as we learned, gets most of its support from outer appearance.

The first room into which we stepped was filled with young S.S. men. their eyes shone with expectation, their ape-like movements betrayed an unhealthy, abnormal sexual excitement. There were also some women in this room, in striped prison clothes, with kerchiefs around their heads. They worked fast, without uttering a word. We did not understand their position, not knowing the hierarchy of Auschwitz, but they were the old prisoners, some of them serving their third or fourth year—the "beauty operators" of the camp.

Coarse voices ordered us to undress. Some of us obeyed automatically, too exhausted to resist. Soon we stood naked, our clothes in a heap around our feet. Some of us protested, but our protests were soon stilled by blows and cruel kicks. There was no escape. In a few short minutes modesty, which had been drilled into us by generations of parents and educators, became a thing of the past. The many women, young and old, ugly and beautiful, undernourished and well-fed, stood defenseless, naked, in a row, exposing their bodies to the curious, hungry eyes of the perverted, depraved thugs who represented Germany's pride.

The floor was littered with dresses, coats, underwear and many lovely things so essential to true femininity. The workers picked up the shoes, stockings, clothes, and hur-´

ried with them to the stock-rooms to sort them and put them in their places.

When we entered the second room we had nothing left of our former identity except our naked bodies and disturbed souls. This room was noisier than the first one, manned by S.S. women who directed the ruthless disfiguring work done by prisoners.

There were dirty, low stools along the walls, and the naked women had to sit down on them, with their backs toward the room, waiting for the next indignity to be inflicted upon them. A moment later we felt the heavy, blunt shears in our hair, and when we looked up again we hardly knew one another any longer. The floor was covered with clouds of silky hair, blond, dark, red, smooth and wavy, short and long; but our heads had acquired a nightmarish appearance, cropped close by unskilled hands, so horrible to look at that we did not know whether to laugh or to cry.

There lay the crown of our female beauty, our hair, to be shipped to Germany for use in the important war industries.

The next room was filled with a burning, acid smell, which made us cry even before we knew what was going to happen to us. The workers smeared on our bodies some strong, smelly liquid, allegedly against lice, which burned sores into our skin and inflicted an excruciating pain on our freshly cropped heads. We had nothing to dry our tears with, and the S.S. men and women were greatly amused by our flowing tears.

The room after this was the shower room. It was so crowded that we could hardly move, and innumerable blows and kicks pressed us even closer together to make room for more women waiting outside. The cold water felt wonderful on our bodies, reminding us of our past, when bathrooms and showers were integral parts of our life and the water supply was unlimited.

But we were given no time to enjoy the blessing of fresh water. Quickly, quickly, we had to leave the room, to go, still wet and shivering, into the next one, where we were to obtain our prison garb.

Long after this first day had become a memory, after weeks and months spent in cold and hunger on the dirty boards of the barracks, I was still trying to figure out the reason for the refined cruelty of our captors. There were mountains of clothes in the warehouses of Auschwitz, the clothes of the murdered victims, our own clothes, the clothes we brought along with us—yet we were given rags. And what horrible, filthy rags!

First we were given a coarse linen shirt, dirty, torn, very old. Then came the dress, if it could be called that. One had to see and wear those dresses to be able to believe that such things really existed. Some were in loud colors, some black, they were made of tulle, silk, or velvet, mostly they were old party dresses now dirty, torn, completely useless. Some consisted of a silk or velvet bodice attached to a short, narrow cotton skirt which barely covered the knees. There were old army trousers sewn together with a red silk blouse, and long tulle dance skirts with a tight, heavy old tweed bodice. Everything was filthy and full of lice and none of it fitted us, as if they had deliberately given clothes too small or too big to everybody. The back of every garment had a big red cross painted on it, extending from the neck all the way to the hem.

We put them on quickly, because we were cold, and then hurried to get a pair of shoes for our freezing feet. The lucky ones got real shoes, but most of us were given a pair of Dutch wooden shoes, which later broke the skin of our feet and caused severe infections. These infections were reason enough to be sent to the crematory, and this is why we were given them in the first place.

But even those who received real shoes were to pay heavily for the privilege. The S.S. men and women were careful never to give a whole pair to anyone. If one of the shoes was a woman's shoe, the victim received a man's shoe for her other foot. If the right shoe was a white sneaker, she was given a high-heeled dance slipper for her left foot. The color, the style, the material was never the same for both feet, because if it had been it could have saved the victim from the crematory and that was not what the Nazis wanted.

When we finally emerged at the other end of the "beauty parlor" building, the street looked like a ghostly carnival. Sisters, friends did not recognize each other any longer, and the prettiest girls and most beautiful women looked like a bunch of grisly monsters, ridiculous, and sub-human.

The clothes we received the first day had to cover our bodies for many long months to come. The cold, the heat, the rain and snow left their marks on them. They grew thinner and more ragged all the time, until they hardly afforded any protection at all. Lice made their home in their folds and they were stained with blood and pus coming from the infected sores which covered our bodies. We worked and slept and ate and stood roll call in them and wore them to the entrance of the crematory, where they were ripped off our bodies to clothe the next group of new arrivals.

And all the time the warehouses of Auschwitz were full of the best, most expensive clothes, and the S.S. women walked among us in brilliant silk dresses, warm coats, their hair newly waved, fragrant with good soap and perfume, laughing at us, torturing us, and deciding which of us should die, which of us should live...

# AUSCHWITZ TREASURE-TROVE
## JULIKA FARKAS

Those who ever believed that organized murder served only to satisfy Nazi perversion would have certainly changed their minds had they spent one day in the stock-rooms attached to the crematories of Auschwitz. There was not one single item on the European market, be it food-stuffs, household goods, luxury articles, cosmetics, tools or dress materials, that could not be found in large quantities in those stock-rooms. No, Auschwitz was not only a play-ground for perverts; it was also a treasure-trove which supplied the German civilians with everything their hearts desired.

A detachment of two hundred prisoners was assigned to the crematory. It was their duty to separate the different kinds of articles and place them on the numerous shelves lining the walls of the huge buildings. Whoever was sent to work there knew that his days were numbered. After eight to ten weeks of this heartbreaking activity they were shot and thrown into the flames.

There were shelves and shelves heavy with blankets of all kinds, beautiful silken ones, woolen ones, featherbeds, and lovely, colorful quilts. There were shelves full of

canned meat, vegetables, fruit, and sweets; there were large
metal boxes full of the most expensive medical instruments
and indescribable riches of drugs which could have saved
our lives if we had only been able to put our hands on
them.

When the ghettos of the various European countries
were evacuated, the inhabitants had no idea where they
were being taken. As every member of the family was permitted to take about fifteen pounds of luggage with him,
everyone took what he valued most or what he thought
would be most needed. Doctors were told to bring their
instruments as they would be permitted to practice their
profession among the Jews. This is how I happened to
bring along my best instruments and most expensive
drugs, which were taken away from me as I entered the
gates of Auschwitz.

In addition to what we were permitted to take, each of
us tried to smuggle in something hidden in our clothes,
sewed into the lining of our coats, so as to have something
to sell, something to give away should our life depend on
our capacity to bribe.

While doing an errand near the crematory one day I
went into the stock-room reserved for children's clothes.
Old prisoners were working here, separating the boys'
clothes from girls' clothes, shoes from stockings, underwear from dresses and the various types of toys from one
another to pack them all in Red Cross packages and send
them to Germany to clothe and amuse the children of good
Nazis. One of the prisoners working there, an eighteen-
year old French girl, Jeanette, could stand this life no
longer and with a piece of glass found on the ground she

cut the veins on both arms. She collapsed, bleeding and I hurried to bandage her arms so as to save her life, if possible, although she would probably have been better off dead. To ease her position I grabbed a small girls' coat lying nearby and put it under Jeanette's head. As I turned the coat inside out I saw a white label sewn into its lining: "I AM JULIKA FARKAS, AGE FIVE. MY FATHER IS DESIDER FARKAS FROM MARAMAROS SZIGET."

The white label of this fine, light-blue coat had a long story to tell. It told me of a blond, blue-eyed little girl, the pride and happiness of her parents, who was one day picked up by cruel Nazi hands and thrown into a cattle car together with her father and mother. During the long trip to Auschwitz little Julika was hungry and thirsty, she cried bitterly in her mother's arms, asking for her soft bed, for her warm milk, for a tender word of comfort and love. But mother had lost her power to comfort her child. She could do nothing but hold her close to her heart, stroke the soft, blond hair and kiss the tear-filled eyes. And even that not for long...

After eight days the journey came to an end at the gates of Auschwitz. Julika was torn from her mother's arms, undressed and thrown into a ditch to be burned alive together with hundreds and hundreds of little boys and girls. Her mother was spared the torture of remembering her child's fate. She went straight to the gas-chambers and found forgetfulness at the merciful hands of death... And now this little blue coat waited to be sent to Germany to clothe another blue-eyed child—perhaps the daughter of her Nazi murderer...

The shelves holding boys' clothing had another story

to tell. When we first arrived at Auschwitz, children under sixteen, whether boys or girls, were permitted to accompany their mothers to the women's camps. Then, as usual, there came a counter-order, and all children of fourteen, fifteen and sixteen had to come forward because they were going to be put into a separate children's camp and receive double bread rations. Gymnastics teachers were told to come forward, too. They would go with the children and teach them physical culture. We were happy. We thought that the children would be used to work and thus escape the unavoidable death by starvation, disease, or burning which awaited them in Auschwitz.

The boys left first. They were kept in a camp near ours and we were able to watch them exercise from morning till night, tired, weak and thin—without the double bread ration they were promised. Then, one night the most horrible screams woke our camp from its deathlike sleep. We ran to the entrance of the camp and witnessed a sight I shall never forget as long as I live.

Several black trucks were standing before the entrance of the boys' camp and a detachment of S.S. men were throwing the naked, crying, screaming little boys on the trucks. Those who tried to escape were dragged back by the hair, beaten with truncheons and whipped mercilessly. There was no help, no escape. Neither their mothers nor God could reach out a helping hand to save their lives. They were burned alive in those crematories which killed and smoked incessantly, day and night.

First they had to exercise to become stronger and "more beautiful" and then they were all murdered in one single night. Why? Can anyone answer? Why?

A few days later I had some work to do in the barracks where these children had lived. There, on the thin plank walls they had written their names and the story of their lives—with their own blood—and a last good-bye. They knew they were to die. They knew they were to be burned, young, innocent, the victims of a world whose conscience shall never rest for having permitted these monstrous crimes...

# CHARLOTTE JUNGER

Little Charlotte Junger, at fifteen, was an exceedingly pretty girl. She was the daughter of a doctor in our town, descended from a long line of well-known physicians. Her parents adored her. Nothing was too good for their blond, blue-eyed, lovely child. And the girl deserved their devotion. She was the best student in her class, excellent in music, and possessed a rare gift for the ballet. Her teachers predicted that she would have a great future in dancing. Her sweetness, her charm endeared her to everyone and she was the first love of my son, to whom music and rhythm had heretofore meant more than anything in the world.

Charlotte Junger led a happy life until the day the Gestapo broke into their home to arrest her parents and herself—an arrest which was to spell their doom. Dr. Junger, who had heard about the atrocities committed in the German concentration camps, had prepared for this eventuality. As the Germans were forcing their way into their home, he seized the hypodermic which he kept handy at all times and injected poison into the arms of his wife and daughter, then emptied the syringe into his own veins. Both he and his wife died almost immediately but, perhaps because of her youth and greater resistance, or maybe because the injection was administered so hurriedly that the needle did not fully penetrate her vein, Charlotte was still alive when they pushed her into the cattle car. During eight days, pressed between terror-sticken children and adults, she suffered the indescribable agonies of slow death. Yet, she was still alive when the contingent of victims arrived at Auschwitz, and with the help of others she succeeded in hiding her precarious state from the Nazis. She was sent "right" and assigned to my block.

Without drugs, without instruments, there was nothing I could do for the child except to hold her in my arms at night and give her small comfort of love and tenderness. Gradually, as the poison invaded her entire system, her ankles and wrists swelled, her cheeks burned red and her blue eyes gleamed steely with fever. I took her to the hospital and watched her condition grow steadily worse. Slowly, inexorably, she was going insane. The moment we left her unguarded, she jumped up from the floor where she lay and began to dance. Gracefully, although her ravaged young beauty was unbearably pathetic, she held out her rags as if they were the lovely white tulle gown she had owned in the past, lifted her swollen little feet and danced...danced.

"Daddy," she whispered, "Daddy, am I going well? Am I making progress? Watch me, Daddy... Do you like this new dance I have learned?"

When Dr. Mengerle heard about the dancing girl, he asked to see her. Day after day he came to watch the dying child perform her complicated dance steps until she collapsed with exhaustion, deathly pale, foaming at the mouth. He pretended that he was her beloved "Daddy," spoke to her kindly and praised her work. In her clouded mind the little girl responded to this travesty and answered him in her perfect German.

Then, one day, Dr. Mengerle tired of Charlotte's dancing. He craved new amusement, new thrills, and the unusual child who was born for happiness and success was pushed into a Red Cross ambulance and carted off to the crematory, where the weak paid the penalty for the sin of being weak...

# THE VALUE OF
# A PIECE OF STRING...

One day followed another in a horrible, nerve-racking monotony and the third month of my stay in Auschwitz arrived without my even being aware of it. We had long ago lost track of time, holding on in our minds to the past, the only escape from insanity. We sank deeper and deeper into the sub-human existence where filth, pain, and crime were natural, and a decent impulse, a human gesture something to be sneered at and disbelieved. I knew that I had died on that March 19, when the Germans overran Hungary and compelled us to give up everything that meant anything to us, pushing us into a ghetto first, then robbing us of possessions, freedom and finally even of human dignity, in this seething, crawling, burning inferno. Here I was only a shadow without identity, alive only by the power of suffering.

It took a piece of string to shake me out of my apathy and remind me that while there was one single breath in me I could not permit myself to be engulfed in this swamp of human depravity.

For two months I had stood on my bare feet during the two daily roll calls. I had no shoes. My feet swelled up

55

and were covered with sores—which was not only painful but also dangerous. Sore feet were reason enough for our Dr. Mengerle to send us to the crematory. I had to have shoes…shoes at any price… Then one of the women working near the crematory stole a pair of shoes for me in exchange for my two days' bread ration. Hunger was not new to me, in a way, I had become accustomed to it, and after only two months at Auschwitz my strength was still holding out—but shoes were a question of life and death.

I received a pair of men's shoes, about size ten, and I refused to listen when they tried to tell me the story of the man who had worn them, maybe not so long ago… I was happy. My aching feet were protected from the mud, the sharp gravel and the filth covering everything. They could rest in those shoes and heal in peace. But my happiness did not last long. The shoes were so big that I could not walk in them. I needed shoe strings. A piece of ordinary string. Anything to keep those shoes on my feet…

The thought of string filled my dreams and every minute of my waking hours. I wanted it so much, so desperately that nothing else seemed to matter anymore. A piece of string…

And then one of my acquaintances told me jubilantly that a few old prisoners, Polish men, were working around the latrines, and one of them had a piece of string…I snatched up my bread ration for the day and ran. The man with the string, my prospective savior, was a short, stocky, pock-marked man with wild eyes and a ferocious expression. The Inferno Auschwitz had succeeded in depriving him of his last vestige of human dignity.

I stopped beside him, held out my bread and asked

him, begged him to give me a piece of string in exchange for it. He looked me over from head to foot, carefully, then grabbed me by the shoulder and hissed in my ear: "I don't want your bread...You can keep your bread...I will give you a piece of string but first I want you...you..."

For a second I didn't understand what he meant. I asked him again, smiling, gently, to give me a piece of string... My feet were killing me... The shoes were useless without string... It might save my life...

He wasn't listening to me. "Hurry up...hurry up..." he said hoarsely. His hand, filthy with the human excrement he was working in, reached out for my womanhood, rudely, insistently.

The next moment I was running, running away from that man, away from the indignity that had been inflicted on me, forgetting about the string, about the shoes, about everything but the sudden realization of how deeply I had sunk... How my values had changed... How high the price of a piece of string had soared...

I sank down on my bunk, dazed with suffering and fear...but a moment later I was on my feet again. No! I would not let this happen to me! I would come out of the apathy which had enveloped me for the last two months and show the Nazis, show my fellow prisoners that we could keep our human dignity in the face of every humiliation, every torture... Yes, I was going to remain a human being to the last minute of my life—whenever that would come.

The same evening, after retiring to our bunks, I began to put my plan into effect. Instead of going to sleep as usual, I began talking in a low voice to the women lying close to me. I told them about my old life in Maramaros

Sziget, about my work, my husband, my son, the things we used to do, the books we used to read, the music we used to listen to... To my surprise they listened with rapt attention, which proved that their souls, their minds were just as hungry for conversation, for companionship, for self-expression as mine. One after the other, they opened up their hearts, and from then on half our nights were spent in conversation.

Later, as we came to know one another better, we invented games to keep our minds off the sordid present. We recited poetry, told stories of the books we had read and liked, and sang songs, in a low voice, with tears in our eyes, careful that the Blockova shouldn't hear us.

Other evenings we played another game, which spread from block to block until every woman in Auschwitz played it enthusiastically. We called the game "I am a lady..."

I am a lady—I said one night—a lady doctor in Hungary. It is morning, a beautiful, sunny morning and I feel too lazy to work. I ring for my assistant and tell her to send the patients away, for I am not going to my office today... What should I do with myself? Go shopping? Go to the hairdresser? Meet my friends at the café? Maybe I'll do some shopping. I haven't had a new dress, a new hat in weeks...

And I went shopping and lunching and walking, went to the theatre with my husband and son, had supper afterwards... And my fellow prisoners hung on my every word, following me around that little town they had never seen, and when my happy, lovely day was over, they fell asleep with a smile on their faces.

These evenings acted like a stimulant. They reminded us that although the odds were all against us, it was still our duty to fight. We had no longer homes to defend. All we had was our human dignity, which was our home, our pride, our only possession—and the moral strength to defend it with.

# IRMA GREZE

Irma Greze was sentenced by the British "to be hanged by the neck until dead." The sentence was executed, but this act of "justice" (real justice would have called for her dying again and again, for every life she had destroyed, or her being tortured and mutilated, for every victim she had tortured and mutilated) will not bring back the dead and neither will it restore to health those whom she had driven to insanity or maimed for life.

She was one of the most beautiful women I have ever seen. Her body was perfect in every line, her face clear and angelic and her blue eyes the gayest, the most innocent eyes one can imagine. And yet, Irma Greze was the most depraved, cruel, imaginative sexual pervert I ever came across. She was the highest ranking S.S. woman in Auschwitz and it was my bad luck to be under her eyes during my entire camp life.

One day she happened to visit the hospital while I was performing an operation on a young woman's breast, cut open by whipping and subsequently infected. I had no instruments whatsoever, except a knife which I had to sharpen on a stone. Breast operations are particularly painful, and, as there was not a drop of anesthetic in this mock hospital, my patient screamed with pain all through the operation.

Irma Greze put down her whip, the handle of which was inlaid with colored beads, sat down on the corner of the bench with served as an operating table and watched me plunge my knife into the infected breast which spurted blood and pus in every direction.

I happened to look up and encountered the most horrible sight I have ever seen, the memory of which will haunt me for the rest of my life. Irma Greze was enjoying the sight of this human suffering. Her tense body swung back and forth in a revealing, rhythmical motion. Her cheeks were flushed and her wide-open eyes had the rigid, staring look of complete sexual paroxysm.

From that day on she went around in camp, her bejewelled whip poised, picked out the most beautiful young women and slashed their breasts open with the braided wire end of her whip. Subsequently those breasts got infected by lice and dirt which invaded every nook and corner of the camp. They had to be cut open, if the patient was to be saved. Irma Greze invariably arrived to watch the operation, kicking the victim if her screams interfered with her pleasure and giving herself completely to the orgastic spasms which shook her entire body and made saliva run down from the corner of her mouth.

One day she ordered me to report to her in the afternoon at the so-called "maternity ward" of our hospital.

"I have watched you operate," she said, "and I have perfect confidence in you as a doctor. I want you to examine me. I think I may be pregnant..."

I knew that it was against the rules for a prisoner to

touch a guard, and breaking that rule was punishable by death. At the same time, refusing an order was punishable by death, too. She lay down on the bench and I proceeded with the examination. She was, indeed, pregnant.

"Be here tomorrow afternoon," she ordered. "You are going to perform an abortion on me..."

But I have absolutely no instruments," I replied "and if someone finds out, that will mean death for me..."

"No arguments. Leave everything to me..."

Next afternoon, at the appointed hour, I was ready, waiting for her. When she arrived, she brought a case of instruments—and her gun.

"They are sterilized," she said handing me the instruments. Then she lay down on the bench and put the gun under her head.

I knelt down on the floor and began to operate. There was absolutely no doubt in my mind that this was going to be the last professional act of my life. We were both breaking the rules. Should anyone find out about it, it would mean the end of her career as an S.S. woman. I would be sent "left"...We were both equally guilty in the eyes of her superiors, yet she held all the cards. No one besides me needed to know about it. She could easily kill me without even having to make an excuse or give an explanation. I was sure that this was what she intended to do.

While my hand worked almost mechanically, my mind was busy with the thought of death. I had often wondered, while reading about a condemned man's last seconds before death, whether it was true that his whole life unfolds before his eyes in a flash. Yes, it is true. I finished the operation and sat back on my heels, too weary even to get up and face death standing. Suddenly I remembered the examination at the end of my first year of high school. I had to figure out how old I was by subtracting the date of my birth from the date of the current year. Then, one picture followed another, until I relived, if not every incident, at least the mood and color of my entire life. It had been a happy life. Happy, successful, filled with love and work which satisfied me completely. I had lost everything, and there was nothing more to live for.

Irma Greze got up from the bench, arranged her clothes, picked up her gun and smiled. I looked up into her smiling face and waited for the bullet which was to put an end to the Dr. Gisella Perl I had been before and to Prisoner No. 25,404 I was now. But she did not shoot.

"You are a good doctor," she said. "What a pity that you have to die. Germany needs good doctors..." I said nothing.

"I am going to give you a coat," she continued. "And I don't have to tell you to keep quiet about this. If you ever open your mouth, I'll find you, wherever you are, and kill you..."

With this she walked out of the shack and left me alone with my newly-won-life. Now, that I knew I wasn't going to die, at least not right then, I remembered my sick and wounded lying on the bare floor of the hospital...I remembered all the pregnant women in camp whose life depended on my skill, courage and readiness to help...and suddenly I knew why I had been spared. I was responsible for those women…I had to remain alive so as to save them from death…I was their doctor…

By-the-way, I never got the coat Irma Greze promised me.

# "CONCERT" IN AUSCHWITZ

Summer 1944... The fine ashes that covered the ground around the four crematories were hot under our bare feet like the sand of the beaches under the feet where free people were spending their vacation.

The thirty-two thousand Polish and Hungarian women inhabiting Block C could hardly remember what free, human life was like. We lost track of time as one hateful day slipped into another. Roll call—rest period. Roll call —sleep. Endlessly. Only the new and ever horrors created by the tireless imagination of our jailers kept torture from becoming a routine.

Our faces were pasty grey in spite of the scorching sun and in spite of our unceasing effort to keep our cheeks pink by pinching them by the hour so that Dr. Mengerle should not find us too sickly to live and send us "left." We had given up the hopeless fight against lice, and our skin was full of infected sores from scratching with dirty fingernails. Washing was a beautiful memory from a past life which, it seemed, had never existed. There was one watertap for all of us, and we were permitted to use it for only two hours a day. Those two hours were spent fighting for a few drops of water to drink and afterwards I had to use my medical skill bandaging broken arms, bleeding scratches, and cracked skulls. We were constantly thirsty, as the turnip soup which made up our main meal was seasoned with saltpeter which was intended to destroy our sex organs. The strong, acid drug burned through the walls of our stomachs and intestines, causing a disease resembling dysentery. Our stomachs were bloated and the complete lack of vitamins dug deep holes into our swollen extremities. There was an epidemic of trenchmouth among us and our bleeding gums made it impossible to chew the hard bread which stood between us and starvation.

We were so weak that we could hardly crawl, yet fear gave us the moral strength to stand at attention four to five hours at dawn and again in the afternoon for roll call. Those who collapsed and those who failed to report were immediately cremated. To save one another's life we dragged the sick, the dying along with us and held them up through those endless hours of numb, bestial suffering.

When Tishah b'ab came, one of the greatest Jewish holidays, our torturers invented a new game to celebrate the day. After the first roll call, which had lasted from the break of dawn to late into the morning, we hardly crawled back into our cage to rest our weary feet and gather strength for the remainder of the day, when we were chased out into the open and ordered to sit in the ashes, which, we were repeatedly told, were the last remains of our parents, husbands, children. They were going to give us a concert...

The smiling, freshly-shaved S.S. men in their gleaming uniforms and the well-fed, well-rested S.S. women with their faces carefully made up, brought comfortable chairs for themselves and sat down in front of the thirty-two thousand walking skeletons who waited, without a sound, for what was to come. A group of prisoners in striped garb came marching toward the platform erected in the middle of the square between the blocks, each carrying a different musical instrument.

They took their places, standing up of course, and began to play. From then on until late at night they played gaudy songs, stirring, exciting, sexy melodies, music that spoke to the body, not the soul, while the four crematories turned living flesh into grey ashes. Ten thousand persons were burned in each of the furnaces that day. The unceasingly dancing flames were brighter and hotter than the sun; heavy smoke filled our nostrils, and thick, black soot settled over the motionless multitude while the expressionless faces of the thirty-two thousand defeated women, whose sorrow was far beyond the comfort of tears, registered nothing but blank despair.

# MARGARINE

The first weeks at Auschwitz were made unbearably miserable by the various skin eruptions caused by the weather, exposure, deficient food and lack of water for drinking and washing. The lice-plague made these eruptions more serious. We scratched in our sleep even if we were strong enough to refrain from it while awake and the sores became infected until our whole body was covered with deep, crater-like wounds.

The fact that I had to stand by and watch while helpless women around me lost first their health, and, as a consequence, their lives, made me deeply miserable. But there was nothing I could do for them without drugs, medicines, salves, bandages and medical instruments. And then, one day, I had an inspiration. I declared, very authoritatively, that margarine was the best medicine against all kinds of skin diseases. We must save our margarine rations and use them on our bodies...Some believed me implicitly, for wasn't I a doctor and supposed to know such things? Others just smiled or sneered. But when those who used this new salve began to get better, the fame of margarine spread all over the camp and even the most cynical tried it out, saying that, after all, it could do no harm...

By some miracle, psychological rather than physiological, the sores healed, no new eruptions occurred and the value of margarine soared to an unbelievable height. Margarine became the highest priced article in Auschwitz, more expensive than bread, clothing, shoes...The latrine, our stock-exchange, was constantly crowded with women who gave away their most highly valued possessions for a dab of margarine. I kept on encouraging this new faith, explaining to them that I was going to patent this new discovery of mine as soon as we got out of Auschwitz...I was going to make millions on it! Such a simple device! How strange that no one ever discovered it... But of course, it is always the simplest things that make most money...

I continued the use of this miracle-salve even after the sign *Hospital* was nailed over the entrance of Block No. 15. That sign kept me from eating and sleeping; I was trembling with excitement, with hope...Everything will be better now—I thought—we have a hospital for our sick, where they will be cured instead of being sent to the crematory. I'll be a doctor again, a healer, a reliever of human suffering.

There were five of us doctors and four nurses. But only the medical staff was real in this new, ghastly Nazi joke. The cages along the walls were soon filled with cases of typhoid, malaria, scarlet fever, pneumonia, contagious skin diseases and insanity, in an unholy medley, where instead of being cured of one disease the patients caught all the other diseases rampant in the camp. We were given no medicines, no bandages except for a few rolls of paper bandage, no instruments. The fever-ridden patients shiv-

ered on the bare planks without blankets; lice crawled over
their bodies carrying germs from one to the other.

One corner of the block was separated from the rest
by a few planks. This corner, with a low, wooden table in it,
was our operating room. This is where we bandaged broken heads and limbs, opened up pussy sores, took blood
tests and pulled infected teeth. The operations were performed with a few pairs of rusty, little scissors, and a knife
which I had to sharpen on a stone. We had no anesthetics,
of course, and the screams of the unfortunate patients
seemed to give Dr. Mengerle a perverse pleasure. He came
to visit the hospital every day and the staff was beaten cruelly, in front of the patients, if the walls were not freshly
white-washed and the floor swept clean with our bare
hands, as we had no broom. The sick could rot in their
skins, but the walls had to be whitewashed.

Still, some of the sick left the hospital cured, more by
being excused from roll call than through treatment. The
hospital also gave me an opportunity to hide the pregnant
until I could interrupt their pregnancy and send them
back to work. The little help I could give, mental as well as
physical, made me forget my troubles and gave a "raison
d'être"—until one day when Dr. Mengerle came charging
into the hospital, with his henchmen behind him, to drag
the sick out of their cages and send them all, without
exception, to the burning furnaces.

From then on I did all I could to keep the sick out of
the hospital. Sore throats, flu, and even pneumonia were
permissible diseases which did not condemn the victim to
immediate execution. But skin diseases, typhoid, malaria

and insanity were to be cured by the flames of the crematory.

When the order came that pregnancy was no longer punishable by death but had to be interrupted and the embryo delivered to Dr. Mengerle for experiments, I was happy again. I could now officially save the lives of pregnant women under slightly better conditions than the filthy floor of the dark barracks.

# BLOCK VII: THE LATRINE

Before we knew what went on in there, it was the ardent desire of all of us to be admitted to Block VII. This block was considerably cleaner, and better built than the others. Rain did not seep through the roof, the cages were more solid and even the air was cleaner. Block VII was the "Worker Block" and it housed fewer women than the others.

One morning a group of unknown S.S. officers and women appeared at the morning roll call. Their visit resulted in a new kind of "selection," in which the young, the pretty, the well-built were pulled out of the ranks, not the weak, the old and the sick-looking. Out of the thirty thousand inhabitants of Camp C about seven hundred young women were selected. The others watched in silence, not knowing whether to pity or envy the chosen ones. We followed them with our eyes and saw that they were being herded into Block VII, the Worker Block.

The camp was soon seething with rumors. We heard that somewhere, far away, there was a radio factory in the middle of a forest and that's where these women would go to work. We did not know that the story about the radio factory was carefully planted among us. We did not know that all these fairy tales about the privileges accorded to those who were taken away for work were only part of the ghastly joke played on us.

About four weeks later an S.S. physician came to Camp C and with a group of strong-armed S.S. men entered Block VII and locked the door from the inside. No one was permitted to go near the block. We still had no idea of what was happening, but waited with fear and curiosity in our hearts.

A few hours later the doctors of the hospital were sent for. The sight which greeted us when we entered Block VII is one never to be forgotten. From the cages along the walls about six hundred panic-stricken, trembling young women were looking at us with silent pleading in their eyes. The other hundred were lying on the ground, pale, faint, bleeding. Their pulse was almost inaudible, their breathing strained and deep rivers of blood were flowing around their bodies. Big strong S.S. men were going from one to the other sticking tremendous needles into their veins and robbing their undernourished, emaciated bodies of their last drop of blood. The German army needed blood plasma! The guinea pigs of Auschwitz were just the people to furnish that plasma. *Rassenschande* or contamination with "inferior Jewish blood" was forgotten. We were too "inferior" to live, but not too inferior to keep the German army alive with our blood. Besides, nobody would know. The blood donors, along with other prisoners of Auschwitz would never live to tell their tale. By the end of the war fat wheat would grow out of their ashes and the soap made of their bodies would be used to wash the laundry of the returning German heroes...

We were ordered to put these women back on their feet before they returned to camp so as to make place for others. What could we do without disinfectants, medicines, liquids? How could we replace the brutally stolen blood? All we had were words, encouragement, tenderness. And yet, under our care, these unfortunate creatures slowly returned to life and they even smiled when saying: "This is still better than the crematory..."

Block VII was always full. Once it was the women with beautiful eyes who were told to come forward, once the women with beautiful hands... And the poor wretches always believed the stories they were told, came forward, and to the amusement of the S.S. henchmen gave their last drops of precious blood for the German soldiers who used the strength robbed from us to murder our friends, our relatives, our allies...

One of the basic Nazi aims was to demoralize, humiliate, ruin us, not only physically but also spiritually. They did everything in their power to push us into the bottomless depths of degradation. Their spies were constantly among us to keep them informed about every thought, every feeling, every reaction we had, and one never knew who was one of their agents.

There was only one law in Auschwitz—the law of the jungle—the law of self-preservation. Women who in their former lives were decent self-respecting human beings now stole, lied, spied, beat the others and—if necessary— killed them, in order to save their miserable lives. Stealing became an art, a virtue, something to be proud of. We called it "organization." Those who were working near the crematories had an opportunity to "organize" an occasional can of food, a pair of shoes, a dress, a cooking pot, a comb, which they then sold on the black market operating in the latrine for food, for special favors, and—if the buyers were men—for "love."

But among those who had no connections among the crematory workers there were many who "organized" the piece of bread of their neighbor, regardless of whether she might starve to death as a consequence, or "organized" their bedfellow's shoes, no matter if her bleeding feet would condemn her to be cremated. By stealing bread, shoes, water, you stole a life for yourself, even if it was at the expense of other lives. Only the strong, the cruel, the merciless survived. The S.S. were, of course, greatly amused by these practices and encouraged them by showing special favors to some, so as to awaken the jealousy, the hatred, the greed of others.

A few privileged persons were tacitly permitted to own small aluminum drinking cups stolen from the crematory. Such a cup made it possible for them to get more water than the others who could only drink from their cupped hands. These cups were jealously guarded, their owners carried them on a piece of string tied around their waist. After they filled it with water, they would seek out a quiet corner were they could enjoy their long drink in peace. But more likely than not, they would not succeed. No sooner had they found a lonely spot than one of the strongest, most brutal fellow prisoners, would sneak up behind them, hit them over the head to rob them of their water and their cup. Many survived these attacks, but others, who had a thin skull or had no resistance left, lost their lives for a drink of water and an aluminum cup...

The latrine—without water, of course—was one of the most important places in Camp C. It was our community hall, the center of our social activities and our news-room. In the second month of my stay in Auschwitz the tiny hut which served as a latrine was closed down and a whole block was consecrated to this worthy purpose. Ditches were dug along the walls and wooden planks thrown across the ditches. In the middle of the building ran a wide passage and this is where the latrine superintendents walked up and down with filthy clubs in their hands, hitting those who spent too much time satisfying their urges or talking to their friends.

The latrine was also our black market, our commodity exchange building. Here you could buy bread for your sausage, margarine for your bread, exchange food, shoes, a piece of cloth for "love"... It was here that we made plans for the future, gave expression to our despair, to our thirst for vengeance, our hatred. It was here that we heard all rumors, the good and the bad, and sometimes, miraculously, they proved to be true. Sometimes I feel that if it hadn't been for the latrine we would all have gone crazy in the deadly monotony of camp life.

Once in a while an S.S. woman came to inspect the latrine and chased us out with her whip and gun. Such an inspection had many victims, many casualties, but the next day our club life would continue, as if nothing had happened.

The latrine also served as a "love-nest." It was here that male and female prisoners met for a furtive moment of joyless sexual intercourse in which the body was used as a commodity with which to pay for the badly needed items the men were able to steal from the warehouses. The salt-peter mixed into our food was not strong enough to kill sexual desire. We did not menstruate, but that was more a consequence of psychic trauma caused by the circum-stances we lived in than of saltpeter. Sexual desire was still one of the strongest instincts and there were many who lacked the moral stamina to discipline themselves.

Detachments of male workers came into Camp C almost daily, to clean the latrines, build streets, and patch up leaking roofs. These men were trusted old prisoners who knew everything there was to know about camp life, had connections in the crematories and were masters at "organizing." Their full pockets made them the Don Juans of Camp C. They chose their women among the youngest, the prettiest, the least emaciated prisoners and in a few sec-onds the deal was closed. Openly, shamelessly, the dirty, diseased bodies clung together for a minute or two in the fetid atmosphere of the latrine—and the piece of bread, the comb, the little knife wandered from the pocket of the man into the greedy hands of the woman.

At first I was deeply shocked at these practices. My pride, my integrity as a woman revolted against the very idea. I begged and preached and, when I had my first cases of venereal disease, I even threatened to refuse treatment if they didn't stop prostitution. But later, when I saw that the pieces of bread thus earned saved lives, when I met a young girl whom a pair of shoes, earned in a week of pros-titution, saved from being thrown into the crematory, I began to understand—and to forgive.

Our S.S. guards knew very well what was going on in the latrine. They even knew who was whose "kochana" (lover), and were much amused by it all. They were always amused by what was insane, filthy, bestial, horrible...The man-eating furnaces were burning, their flames were licking the sky... Millions were dying on their feet eaten up alive by lice, hunger, disease—and in the latrines, lying in human excrement before the eyes of their fellow prisoners, men and women were writhing in sexual paroxysm. Hitler's dream of a New Order...

# CHILDBIRTH IN CAMP C

The poor, young women who were brought to Auschwitz from the various ghettos of Hungry did not know that they would have to pay with their lives and the lives of their unborn children for that last, tender night spent in the arms of their husbands.

A few days after the arrival of a new transport, one of the S.S. chiefs would address the women, encouraging the pregnant ones to step forward, because they would be taken to another camp where living conditions were better. He also promised them double bread rations so as to be strong and healthy when the hour of delivery came. Group after group of pregnant women left Camp C. Even I was naive enough, at that time, to believe the Germans, until one day I happened to have an errand near the crematories and saw with my own eyes what was done to these women.

They were surrounded by a group of S.S. men and women, who amused themselves by giving these helpless creatures a taste of hell, after which death was a welcome friend. They were beaten with clubs and whips, torn by dogs, dragged around by the hair and kicked in the stomach with heavy German boots. Then, when they collapsed, they were thrown into the crematory—alive.

I stood, rooted to the ground, unable to move, to scream, to run away. But gradually the horror turned into revolt and this revolt shook me out of my lethargy and gave me a new incentive to live. I had to remain alive. It was up to me to save all the pregnant women in Camp C from this infernal fate. It was up to me to save the life of the mothers, if there was no other way, then by destroying the life of their unborn children. I ran back to camp and going from block to block told the women what I had seen. Never again was anyone to betray their condition. It was to be denied to our last breath, hidden from the S.S., the guards and even the Blockova, on whose good will our life depended.

On dark nights, when everyone else was sleeping—in dark corners of the camp, in the toilet, on the floor, without a drop of water, I delivered their babies. First I took the ninth-month pregnancies, I accelerated the birth by the rupture of membranes, and usually within one or two days spontaneous birth took place without further intervention. Or I produced dilatation with my fingers, inverted the embryo and thus brought it to life. In the dark, always hurried, in the midst of filth and dirt. After the child had been delivered, I quickly bandaged the mother's abdomen and sent her back to work. When possible, I placed her in my hospital, which was in reality just a grim joke. She usually went there with the diagnosis of pneumonia, which was a safe diagnosis, not one that would send her to the crematory. I delivered women pregnant in the eighth, seventh, sixth, fifth month, always in a hurry, always with my five fingers, in the dark, under terrible conditions.

No one will ever know what it meant to me to destroy these babies. After years and years of medical practice, childbirth was still to me the most beautiful, the greatest miracle of nature. I loved those newborn babies not as a doctor but as a mother and it was again and again my own child whom I killed to save the life of a woman. Every time when kneeling down in the mud, dirt and human excrement which covered the floor of the barracks to perform a delivery without instruments, without water, without the most elementary requirements of hygiene, I prayed to god to help me save the mother or I would never touch a pregnant woman again. And if I had not done it, both mother and child would have been cruelly murdered. God was good to me. By a miracle, which to every doctor must sound like a fairy tale, every one of these women recovered and was able to work, which, at least for a while, saved her life.

My first such case was the delivery of a young woman called Yolanda. Yolanda came from my hometown. She was the child of an impoverished family and made a living by doing fine embroidery on expensive underwear, handkerchiefs—and baby clothes. To make beautiful baby clothes was the greatest pleasure in her life and, while working on them until late into the night, she would dream about the baby she, herself, would one day have. Then she got married. Month after month she waited and prayed, but Nature refused to grant her most ardent wish. This is when she began coming to me. I treated her for a long time until finally my treatment showed results and Yolanda became pregnant. She was radiant. "I shall give you the most beautiful present in the world when my baby arrives..." she would then tell me every time we met.

In the end it was I who gave her a present—the present of her life—by destroying her passionately desired little boy two days after his birth. Day after day I watched her condition develop, fearing the moment when it could be hiddened no longer. I bandaged her abdomen, hid her with my body at roll call and hoped for a miracle which would save her and her baby.

The miracle never came, but one horribly dark, stormy night Yolanda began having birthpains. I was beside her, waiting for the moment when I could take a hand in the delivery, when I saw to my horror, that she fell into convulsive seizures. For two days and nights the spasms shook her poor, emaciated little body and I had to stand by, without drugs, without instruments to help her, listening to her moans, helpless. Around us, in the light of a few small candles I could see the thirteen-hundred women of her barracks look down upon us from their cages, thirteen-hundred death-masks with still enough life left in them to feel pity for Yolanda and to breathe the silent but ever-present question: Why?

The third day Yolanda's little boy was born. I put her into the hospital, saying that she had pneumonia—an illness not punishable by death—and hid her child for two days, unable to destroy him. Then I could hide him no longer. I knew that if he were discovered, it would mean death to Yolanda, to myself and to all these pregnant women whom my skill could still save. I took the warm little body in my hands, kissed the smooth face, caressed the long hair—then strangled him and buried his body under a mountain of corpses waiting to be cremated.

Then, one day, Dr. Mengerle came to the hospital and gave a new order. From now on Jewish women could have their children. They were not going to be killed because of their pregnancy. The children, of course, had to be taken to the crematory by me, personally, but the women would be allowed to live. I was jubilant. Women, who delivered in our so-called hospital, on its clean floor, with the help of a few primitive instruments that had been given to me, had a better chance to come out of this death-camp not only alive but in a condition to have other children—later.

I had two hundred ninety-two expectant mothers in my ward when Dr. Mengerle changed his mind. He came roaring into the hospital, whip and revolver in hand, and had all the two hundred ninety-two women loaded on a single truck and tossed—alive—into the flames of the crematory.

In September 1944, Camp C was liquidated to make place for new arrivals. I shall tell later, what this liquidation meant. All I want to say here is that out of thirty thousand women only ten thousand remained alive to be put into other blocks or taken to Germany to work.

As soon as we were installed in Camps F, K and L, a new order came from Berlin. From now on, not only could Jewish mothers have their children in the "maternity ward" of the hospital but the chidren were to be permitted to live.

Eva Benedek was eighteen years old. She was a violinist from Budapest, a beautiful, talented young woman who was separated from her husband only a few days after her wedding. Eva Benedek believed with an unconquerable faith that her life and the life of her child would be saved. The child, growing in her womb, was her only comfort, her only pleasure, her only concern. When the S.S. organized an orchestra among the prisoners Eva became the violinist of that orchestra. I bandaged her abdomen and in her formless rags, amidst women whose stomachs were constantly bloated with undernourishment, her condition went unnoticed.

Then came the "liquidation" of Camp C and Eva Benedek came with me to Camps F, K and L. When the order for the conservation of Jewish children came, nobody was happier than she. Her delivery was only a day or two off and we both believed that the miracle had happened, a miracle of God for the sake of Eva Benedek. She smiled all day and in the evening, in our barracks, she whistled Mozart concertos and Chopin valses for us to bring a little beauty into our terror-filled, hopeless lives.

Two days later she had her baby, a little boy, in the "maternity ward". But when the baby was born, she turned her back on it, wouldn't look at it, wouldn't hold it in her arms. Tears were streaming down her cheeks incessantly, terrible silent tears, but she wouldn't speak to me. Finally I succeeded in making her tell what was on her mind.

"I dare not take my son in my arms, Doctor," she said. "I dare not look at him, I dare not kiss him, I dare not get attached to him. I feel it, I know it, that somehow they are going to take him away from me..."

And she was right. Twenty-four hours after Eva Benedek had her son, a new order came, depriving Jewish mothers of the additional food, a thin, milky soup mixed with flour, which swelled their breasts and enabled them to feed their babies. For eight days Eva Benedek had to look on while her son starved slowly to death.

His fine, white skin turned yellow and blotched, his smooth face got wrinkled and shrivelled and on the eighth day I had to take him out and throw him on a heap of rotting corpses.

# THE HOSPITAL STAFF

When I first met Olga Schwartz, in the spring of 1942, I immediately felt that our friendship was more that just a passing attachment. She was a pediatrician at one of the the Budapest clinics together with my sister Helen. The two of them were very close friends, knew all about each other's background and family, and planned to work together in the future. When I arrived in Budapest to do some work at the clinic and study the new medical methods and discoveries so as to keep up with progress, I was immediately admitted to their circle, of which my son became the fourth member. We spent all our free time together, discussed medicine, read scientific books and in the evenings listened to my son playing the violin.

Olga was a tall, slender, brown-haired, blue-eyed young woman of extraordinary intelligence. She loved her work passionately and, as many doctors do, took a deep interest in music. We spent an unforgettable four weeks in each other's company and we knew that our mutual understanding and affection would last as long as we lived. Later, after I had returned home, Olga married a physician, moved to Cluj, a beautiful city in Transylvania, and gave birth to a little son. Her life, like mine, became gradually more difficult and the things we had to fight, besides misery and disease, became more numerous.

In the spring of 1944 when the Jewish physicians in Camp C were ordered to come forward, I noticed a tall, extremely thin woman with closely cropped hair and large blue eyes. Where had I seen those blue eyes before? I looked at her, she looked at me, and suddenly I felt as if a cruel hand had taken hold of my heart. Olga!

"Be in the latrine after the evening roll call!" I called to her before we were ordered to retire to our blocks. She nodded and I knew that she, too, had recognized me.

After the second roll call we met in the fetid darkness of the latrine. Crying, deeply shaken, we embraced each other. And then we began asking question after question. "Do you know where you are? Do you know the meaning of all this, the fire, the torture, the methodical degradation? Do you understand their aim and do you know our duty?"

"Yes...Yes, Olga, I know it all... I know their aim and I know it is our duty to fight against them, against death, against their power to debase us..."

"Then we'll stick together and fight together..." she said. Solemnly we shook hands and from then on our friendship and common fight became our constant source of strength and endurance during all those infernal months in Auschwitz.

When the Nazis decided to give us a hospital and appointed five doctors and four nurses to tend to the sick, the nine of us made a solemn pact and swore to defeat the Nazis in their attempt at degrading us, debasing us, and breaking our spirit before throwing us into the flames. We all knew that our jailors were not satisfied with beating, starving, torturing our bodies until we looked like walking skeletons covered with sores and our organs were destroyed for ever, that they also wanted to deform our souls. It amused them to watch our gradual deterioration and see how long it took for the most cultured twentieth-century intellectuals to reach the moral standards of a hyena. With infinite cleverness, giving attention even to smallest details, they created a gutter-mentality, a spiritual swamp, a cesspool of corruption among us until the soil was ripe for every kind of crime to mushroom.

Yet they did not succeed completely. Some of their victims' reactions were the opposite of what they had expected. I observed acts of such human greatness, kindness, sacrifice and selflessness that witnessing them made life worth living. Only an inferno like Auschwitz could produce people like Olga, Kati and many others, whose friendship is still my proudest possession.

I shall never forget Kati. She was a strong, simple girl with a heart as big as the universe. I met her one night in the camp streets, bending over the body of a small, human being who was lying in the mud, uttering pitiful, puppy-like short screams and holding out its hands to us. It was a very young girl, about fifteen, who had been beaten to within an inch of her life by one of the S.S. women for trying to find a few potato peelings on the garbage heap behind the kitchen. Kati picked her up, wiped her tears away from the tortured little face and took the child with her into her cage.

From that day on she never left the little girl, provided for her, stole for here and did everything in her power to keep her alive and well. Kati had a very good *kohana*—lover

—a German prisoner who wore a green triangle next to his number on his chest. The green triangle designated the ordinary criminals, thieves, robbers, murderers. Prostitutes had to wear a black triangle, political prisoners a red, and Jews a yellow one. It caused Olga and me much bitter amusement that the Nazis, the world's greatest criminals and mass murderers, should punish a man who killed not more than one or two people in his life. The murder of one single human being rated only a green triangle, but the murder of millions rated an elegant S.S. uniform...

Kati's German was a big, strong man with a heavy cane that symbolized his elevated status. A cane meant rank, position, power. It meant more than a baronetcy or a knighthood. Kati was just about to break off this relationship when she came upon the little girl, but now she decided to continue selling her body to the man in exchange for food which she then took back to the cage and fed to the little girl. Kati was only happy when the child had enough to eat. The German had good connections at the crematory and consequently Kati's little protégé had everything her heart desired. One day I saw them both in a cattle car carrying workers to Germany. They were holding each other's hands and I knew that whatever the cost, Kati would save the life of that little girl...

The nine members of the hospital staff formed a small oasis in the swamp of misery and crime which was Auschwitz. Their selection was an outcome of Mengerle's whim, but I firmly believe that Fate must have guided his hand. These nine women were nine real human beings. We all had a clear picture of what was going on. We saw things as a whole, and forgot our personal fate in the fight for others. We were the only ones who offered help to the needy by listening to their stories, giving them courage and treating their diseased bodies to the best of our ability.

Doctor Rose—one of my colleagues, who was dying in Block 19 at the time I left Auschwitz—was not only a pediatrician, she was a child herself. Optimism shone like the sun in her eyes. She was always smiling, always joking, always full of hope. She never ate, but day after day one could see her running through Camp C carrying a piece of bread, a cup of soup hidden between her rags, taking it to the sick, the dying. Her laughter was a constant source of joy to all of us and her contempt for those who lost faith kept us often from giving way to despair.

Doctor Charlotte was a symbol of motherly love. She had four sisters with her in Camp C, until one of them was burned alive before her eyes. From then on she kept the other three constantly close to herself, protected them with the fierceness of a tiger, shared her small cot with them, and cleaned them, fed them, nursed them as if she were their mother. She was born to be the mother of many children. Her overflowing affection warmed the entire camp and her patients reciprocated with filial tenderness.

Rose's goodness was more conscious. She was a militant idealist and her every action bore proof to her beliefs. Her moral strength never deserted her, not even later in Belsen Bergen when the hunger and typhus had completely undermined her physical resistance.

And then there were Magda, Minna, Lenore and Suzanne, the four nurses who did the dirty work at the hospital, always smiling, always willing, enduring every hardship with such nobility and uprighteousness which commanded the greatest admiration.

We doctors were often able to get something extra in the way of food. The men from the other camps liked to come to us for treatment and every time they came they brought us something to pay for our services. A small operation, such as opening a cyst or a malignant boil, rated a can of food, a piece of margarine or a few slices of wurst. They were the "private" patients of the hospital. Whatever we received during the day we shared in the evening and thus had enough energy to go on with our work the next day.

Those evenings at the hospital are the only bearable memory of my Auschwitz days. We were nine friends, nine women of the same cultural and social background, with the same interests, the same enthusiasms, the same ideals. We knew what we were living for and we helped one another in our common fight. When we were hungry, we consoled ourselves by talking literature, quoting passages from the works we loved. When we were tired, when Mengerle beat us—to break our spirit—we put our heads together and recited songs of freedom. We did not break … We could not break. We know that thirty-two thousand helpless women needed us.

Sometimes we did not eat the food we earned during the day from our "private" patients. We looked at the bread, the margarine, the wurst hungrily, but refrained from touching it, because one of us needed a pair of shoes, a piece of cloth. One time, I remember, I needed a pair of shoes very badly. But at the same time we were also very hungry. My eight companions were ready to do without the extra food, but day after day I made them eat whatever we received, saying that my shoes could wait...

We all loved one another, but Olga and I meant more to each other than the others meant to us. We shared our cot, our food, our every thought. She protected me and I protected her. She was the only one who knew what I was doing when I sneaked out in the middle of the night to rid pregnant women of their babies and thereby save their lives. She knew, and she trembled for my life. "Take care of yourself..." she admonished me daily. "Don't give too much of yourself... You'll only wear out your heart..."

Olga was the best, the most wonderful human being I ever met. And she was also an excellent physician with a vast store of knowledge. Whenever we had a more interesting medical case, we used to discuss it for hours, treating it in theory as if we were back at the clinic in Budapest. When Dr. Mengerle decided that every feverish patient should have a blood test made to find out whether she had typhoid, we knew that he intended to kill off a new contingent of our patients. What could we do? How should we hide our typhoid cases from him? Up to that day, it had sufficed if we said that the patient had pneumonia, but a Vidal reaction would give us all away... Then Olga had a wonderful idea. Instead of taking blood tests from our typhoid cases, we took samples of each other's blood and gave it to Dr. Mengerle. The tests were negative, and the patients were saved.

But it was not only the typhoid patients Olga saved. Once she had to protect me, in almost the same manner, for four entire weeks. At that time I had an S.S. man as a secret patient whom I had to meet at a certain hour at a certain place. Having been held up by a delivery case, I was late for the appointment and the brute kicked me in the abdomen with his heavy boots until I collapsed in a dead faint. It was Olga who found me, took me back to the hospital and did my work for me until I was strong enough to stand on my feet again. Had Dr. Mengerle known of my condition, he would have sent me to the crematory.

In 1944, Olga was appointed to accompany a big transport of workers to Germany as their physician. We felt that the world had come to an end. We did not want to part, we could not imagine what life would be like without each other. I ran to Dr. Mengerle and begged him almost on my knees to let me go with Olga. The answer was "no." Then Olga went to see him. She offered to denounce her position as a physician and work as a nurse or a cleaning woman if she could only stay with me. He looked us over carefully. He knew what a wonderful physician Olga was and that her profession was the only thing which kept her alive. He understood what this sacrifice meant to her, and yet she wanted to make it. The emotion that passed across his face was unreadable. But the answer was still the same. "You go!" he said to Olga. "You stay!" he said to me. And a little later I saw my best friend, my sister, disappear in the autumn fog, on her feet the black men's shoes I had bought for her with the five portions of margarine I had earned.

In April 1945, after the liberation in Belsen Bergen, a skelton-like man came to see me at the hospital. "Doctor, save me... I am dying... I am Olga's husband." I put my arms around him, crying, and from that day on I nursed him, tended him with the same love I had given to his wife. Neither of us knew where she was. We did not even know whether she was still alive ... When he was strong enough to travel, I sent him with a sick-transport to Sweden to regain his weight and his health.

Several months later, on a hot July day, when I was just recovering from typhus which I had contracted in Belsen Bergen, somebody walked into my room. It was Olga. She had come, on foot, all the way from Prague to look for me in all the camps in Germany. Only then did she learn that her husband was still alive. It made me indescribably happy that it was I who had saved my best friend's husband for her. We spent wonderful four days together and then she left to search for my husband. She never found him. A few days before the liberation, after two years of inhuman suffering, the Nazis had beaten him to death ...

Olga Schwartz and later, in Hamburg, Olga Singer were my most beloved two camp-sisters. The physician and the teacher—two great human beings and the best friends anyone ever had...

# THE STORY OF THE FATAL HANDKERCHIEF

Lily was a great actress, a spoiled and luxury-loving lady. She had walked on the sunny pathways of life. Silks and velvets had covered her smooth skin and her tremendously valuable jewels were safely deposited in a vault in Switzerland. Her warm mezzo soprano voice had enchanted all human hearts. She was beautiful, at the peak of success and the center of public admiration.

A long, long time ago—when her voice came to me through the radio, I would listen in delighted wonder. I would have liked to stretch out my hand to reach her, to touch her, to caress this lovely, glamorous woman, this great artist.

At last, in November of 1943, in Budapest's fashionable Artists Club, where she generally presided over the party, laughing and enjoying life, I was introduced to her and spoke with her for the first time. She believed in American-British victory, she was convinced that Hungary would manage to keep out of this bloody deluge, and that the reign of democracy in which she also staunchly believed would prevail in the not too-distant future. But her serious words were soon interrupted by boisterous, ringing laughter, for she loved and enjoyed life above all.

Summer 1944. Perhaps it was in June. I worked in the "ambulance," a small wooden shed. Jostling each other, my shadow-like fellow-camp inmates waited for "treatment." The air reeked with the penetrating smell of dirty bodies, pus-filled wounds which covered rotting extremities. They all beseech me, pleading for medical care. It is noon. Soon the roll call will sound. They must throng and scamper, for all the wounds must be covered somehow, must be hidden by some bandage by that time. Loud wailing pervades the miasma-filled atmosphere. The lice-infested scratch themselves till they bleed. From time to time some woman rushes in with a head injury, maybe a broken skull; perhaps she was thirsty and wanted a drink, or sought to discharge her needs, or maybe only because of some caprice of an S.S. guard.

It is noon. I have been on my feet since early morning in my six foot wide and nine foot long office. A bench beside the wall keeps some order in this space. Eight to ten patients sit there and twenty to twenty-five more crowd around me.

There is absolutely no air. My lungs hurt at every breath I take and I suffer dreadfully from the impossibility of coping with the situation. I lack bandage material, which at best is paper, through which the putrid flow trickles; a scanty supply of vaseline, some hypermanganese—that is all; and many, many delusive, hollow words of comfort: "This will do now; the wounds will all heal; do not despair." And I speak and speak of the past, because the present is unbearable and there is no future—and the past gives strength to bear all.

Every wound hurts me, too. After every abscess I have to swallow painfully to hide my nausea and my impotent distress—the atrociousness of being a physician in this Nazi hell.

Then I see someone in front of me. Shorn greyish hair-stumps, a pallid, sallow face, her body wrapped in a grey rag held together by a string around her waist. One brown and one black boot on her feet.

"Don't you recognize me, Doctor?" a velvety voice chants. No, this cannot be! Who is this bald, diabolical figure? That unforgettable voice! It can only be...Yes, it is Lily!

I collect my presence of mind; this encounter must not find me like this, with tears in my eyes. I try to smile.

"How beautiful you are even here; what heavenly music, your voice—even here," I tell her. A faint color spreads on her sallow cheeks. "Wait; wait until I finish my work." She stands in the corner to wait.

I seem to see her there now, her head erect, leaning against the wooden wall, hands folded on her wasted body, violet-blue eyes contemplating the morbid scene. Instead of the glamorous golden crown, grey stubs cover her fine, intelligent head. She just stands in the corner lady-like, refined, gentle—for she remained a lady, refined and gentle even here.

Then she tells me that the Gestapo had seized her because she was Jewish, "anglophile" and democratic. Oh! Oh! These are great sins! They slapped her and beat her. She was transported to the distribution camp Kistarcsa, there thrown into a cattle car and thus one dark night landed here in the Auschwitz hell. Here she had been for three weeks, and today had heard of my presence.

"Doctor, help me! I want to live, I want so much to live! I have such faith that these barbed wires will fall, that these gates will open, that we will once more be free. I believe in life, and I want to live! Help me, help me!"

I stroked her hands and we vowed an alliance then and there, in the filthy ambulance; that we would never forsake each other; that we wanted to live and would live. From that time, day after day, when actually not on roll call, she was in my office, standing there in her corner, head leaning against the wall. And I sent her my best smile, the encouragement of my eyes, which convinced her that she was no longer alone.

She became infested with lice, and I produced cream for her. I bandaged her wounded feet the best I could. When she acquired bladder disease, I made a warm padding of paper for her to wear on her abdomen. Every trifle ailment was conscientiously cared for, so that she would feel and know how important her life was.

Perhaps it was not even normal the way this woman clung to life. As a physician I often admired her indomitable life-instinct—at a place where the sky was always aglow from burning human bodies; where life had so little value and security; where everyone yearned for death, this woman kept on being so frantically attached to life. What did it matter if she was covered with lice, if she was hungry, if she was cold? She stood erect at roll call and believed in life.

In Auschwitz there were no handkerchiefs, no towels,

no tooth-brushes—not even a piece of paper. And the lack of these caused so much suffering, so much disaster! (Even today when I hold a handkerchief in my hand, I fondly stroke it and cherish it as the wonderous fulfillment of a deep and great desire).

The camp existence taught us a lot of tricky contrivances. For our noses trickled sometimes, our mouths and teeth were coated with filth every morning, and the lower parts of our bodies had to be cleaned daily. But we had nothing that would serve that purpose. As all who wished to keep alive had to be ingenious, a strange custom continued to prevail in the whole camp—the custom of tearing tiny squares of material off our shirts and using them to clean our bodies.

Lily also soon learned the use of her chemise, the value of the small, torn-off rags. However, towards the end of the summer not much of her chemise was left, for she could not be thrifty. One fine day an S.S. guard accosted her, jerked up her dress and behold, only her shoulder straps were there, with just a strip of the rest of what once was a chemise!

"You revolutionary swine! You thief! Where is the camp chemise?" and blows poured down upon her from whip and stick! When Lily came to me at our daily encounter in the "ambulance," she was covered all over with blood. There she stood waiting in her usual corner and on that day, in my reeking ambulance, she gave her first concert! She sang *La Traviata* heavenly, exquisitely, and I smiled my encouragement more intensely than ever. From that day on I had to take even better care of her.

When autumn came, the camp was to be partly "liquidated." Our S.S. chief, under excuse of "selection," speeded up mass murder. Lily's life became that of a hunted animal. She ran from one block to another. One day Block 28-29 was selected, half of its inmates dispatched to the crematory; so Lily hid and the Russian girl in charge, the Blockova, let her stay there because she sang arias so beautifully. But next day the same block was "selected" again. There was no rest for Lily any more—no rest anywhere.

She wandered from one block to another, singing her arias to obtain right of asylum. But all blocks has a definite and limited number of inmates. She desperately wanted to live, to escape the eyes of Mengerle and his death-dealing hands. But the ring tightened more and more. Hiding became impossible. Lily shrank to a shadow of her former self, of that once lovely woman. What hunger and filth had not been able to destroy, this panic had managed to disintegrate entirely.

Late September. Pouring rain, mud, swamp, engulfing fog. Only the crematory aglow with hellish intensity. Everyone was due to stand at roll call for general "selection."

Where to hide, where to run? Lily awaits help from me and I am helpless myself.

I hide her in my "ambulance." For she wants to live, and knows that if Mengerle sees her wasted, thin, ill body, he will throw her into the flames. There is no mercy! She hides. But the number at roll call does not check. They search for the missing one. And the Blockova finds Lily in her hiding place. That Russian girl is also terrified, since she has to pay with her life for anyone who is missing. Her bestial instincts are aroused. She snatches Lily by the throat, slapping her face right and left. Lily, who had always been a perfect lady, refined and gentle even in hell, now can no longer control herself. She throws off all restraint and thrusts her long, sharp nails into the face of the Blockova, scratching and tearing her, screaming and shouting: "I want to live, I want to live!"

So they drag her before the S.S. guards. They cut her newly grown hair, they tear off all of her rags, till she stands naked in front of all the prisoners. To teach us a lesson, they whip her so that her blood spurts all over us and tear her limbs. She screams and yells like a wild beast when put into the black cart on the way to the fire tomb.

She wanted so much to live. She fought for her life for six months, disciplining herself to the utmost, bearing everything, suffering in silence, even singing—to remain alive! And now, now she, too, was burned! I still hear her lovely voice ...

# ONE WOMAN'S DEATH

The teacher and his family lived at the outskirts of town. The house was a square, white box and its white-curtained windows looked wise and serene, like the eyes of its inhabitants. There were corn fields and undulating wheat fields behind the house, and beyond them—the river. In the distance, like a velvety, green cloud, one could see the oak-covered slopes of the Carpathians, and above the mountains, the cool, blue sky.

The family was happy in this setting of beauty and peace. They did not crave the noise and light of the main street. Each morning the teacher and his wife, who was also a teacher, left the house together to share faith in knowledge, honesty, justice and beauty with the children of the town. They loved their pupils almost as much as they loved their own children, who filled the house with gaiety and promise.

The teachers' children learned the meaning of freedom and democracy early in life. The parents' earnings were hardly sufficient to keep all of them in food and clothing, and the only luxury they knew was culture, the luxury of the mind.

Everybody liked and respected the teacher and his

wife. Their days and years rolled peacefully, filled with work, with love for each other and for their children, and with the satisfaction of duty well done. By the time they retired from teaching to live on their well-earned pension, their sons had left the house to seek work, freedom and happiness in foreign countries, as the conditions in their own country had grown from bad to worse.

Only the five daughters remained at home, waiting for husbands to save them from the idleness imposed upon them by a country that could give employment not even to its male population. Ibi, short for Ibolya, or Violet, was the oldest. She was a tall, well-built, lovely girl, whose most attractive feature was her long, shining black hair, worn in a crown of braids around her head.

In her desperate quest for a husband, Ibi made a habit of reading through the personal ads in the daily paper. One day she found one which appealed to her imagination. "I want to marry an intelligent brunette, who wears her hair in braids around her head," the ad said, and Ibi sat down to write a letter. It did not take long before she got an answer, and a few months later she was married.

However, the charm of the braids wore off in no time, and two years after her wedding Ibi returned to her parents' house, bringing with her her little son. To support herself and her child she opened a dressmaking establishment in town which soon became the best, most sought-after "salon" in the area. She spent all of her free time with her son, whom she adored with all the concentrated emotions of a frustrated woman. Everything would have been well if her divorced husband had not again and again stolen the child whenever Ibi was at work. Several times a year she had to leave her salon, take a train and pursue the man in order to steal back the child.

This went on for years, until one day Ibi found herself behind the barbed wire fences of Auschwitz. Her entire family had been cremated except the child, but about his fate she was kept in ignorance. Her braids had been shaved off, and the well-formed, round head was covered with a strong, greying stubble. Her physical condition deteriorated rapidly, only her soul, her will to live were indestructible. She refused to believe that the bodies of our loved ones were used to make soap and fertilizer for the Germans. She knew that the realization of the cruel truth would deprive her of her inner strength and she wanted to live—for her son…

Ibi stood the two daily roll calls without complaint. She ate the horrible, filthy turnip soup to the last drop, because it stood between her and starvation. She killed off the lice covering her body with infinite patience, fought against disease, weakness, demoralization and hopelessness with the unflagging persistence of a maniac. She even fought, for a while successfully, against death…

At the first "selection" after her arrival, Ibi was singled out by the S.S. physician to die in the flames of the crematory. Maybe it was her tall frame which caught his attention, or maybe it was the burning intelligence and the determination to live which shone in her sunken, beautiful, dark eyes. She was thrown in the rear of the truck, her naked body squeezed in between hundreds of other naked bodies, whose screams and shouts for help, for mercy, filled the air until it penetrated our throats, our lungs, with every breath we took.

But Ibi was not beaten, yet. The terror, which for a moment had paralyzed her brain, gave way to a frantic search for an idea that would save her. The whips of the S.S. guards beat down upon them like hail to silence the desperate screams of the victims and the truck rolled out of the camp towards the crematory, which was to put an end to these young, innocent human lives. A deep silence descended upon the camp and the fear of tomorrow replaced the sorrow we felt for those whose turn had come today.

I was about to lie down on my filthy cot in the hospital, when suddenly, out of the darkness, I saw Ibi appear before me. "I have jumped off the truck..." she related. "They caught me, but they must have been impressed by my courage, or by the way I jumped, because they did not put me back on. They let me go. Please, Doctor, let me stay at the hospital for a few days."

She stayed at the hospital to recover from the "selection" and her desperate jump, until Dr. Mengerle decided to make the hospital the scene of the next selection. He walked through the wards, inquired as to the diagnosis in each case, then called his guards, ordered them to strip the patients and after beating, kicking, whipping them to within an inch of their lives, loaded the entire hospital on a truck and sent them to be cremated. Ibi was among the patients. But again she jumped off the truck and at night was back at the hospital.

In the following six months Ibi was selected to die six times. Every time she returned from the doors leading to the flames, because she wanted to live...because she wanted to find her son... At the last escape she broke her leg. I kept her at the hospital for four weeks, until her leg mended.

Day after day I sat at her bedside talking, feeding her on dreams of the past and the future. This built up the resistance of her spirit and helped her to recover in spite of her terribly weakened condition.

She liked to reminisce on the story of her six escapes and laughed about her newly acquired skill which any circus performer would be proud to possess. She firmly believed that, having survived six death sentences, she was safe and would live to see her son again.

It was Fall by the time her leg had healed—a cold, humid Fall. The rain beat down mercilessly on the ragged skeletons standing at attention during the long hours of the roll call. The liquidation of the camp had begun and the tempo of selection increased.

At one of the roll calls, Dr. Mengerle's eyes alighted on Ibi's silver-stubbled head. "You are still here?" he asked her bitingly. Ibi's pale face grew even paler but she did not answer. Her rags were taken away and she stood trembling, in the long line of naked women flanked by two rows of S.S. guards armed to the teeth. The cold rain drenched the emaciated bodies, their bony feet disappeared in the soft, thick mud and still the order to march did not come. Hours went by, long hours that seemed like years of torture to those who knew what was waiting for them. Whenever one of them screamed or collapsed, the guards would pounce on her and beat her, kick her until she fell silent or dragged herself to her feet...

Then Dr. Mengerle shouted an order, and the column began to move. The naked, helpless women had no more fight left in them. They obeyed automatically, walked without a sound towards the ultimate salvation—towards death...

But again, for the last time, Ibi's terrific will to live asserted itself. She jumped out of the line, and regardless of the armed guards, regardless of the hopelessness of her plight, she began to run. She must have known that there was no place to hide, no possibility to escape, but the thought of her son, of life, was stronger than reason.

Dr. Mengerle left the head of the column and with a few, easy strides, caught up with her. He grabbed her by the neck and proceeded to beat her head into a bloody pulp. He hit her, slapped her, boxed her, always her head, only her head—screaming at her at the top of his voice. "You want to escape, don't you...You can't escape now...This is no truck, you can't jump...You going to burn like the others...You are going to croak, you dirty Jew..." And he went on hitting the poor, unprotected head.

As I watched, I saw her two beautiful, intelligent eyes disappear under a layer of blood... Her ears weren't there any longer, maybe he had torn them off... And in a few seconds her straight, pointed nose was a flat, broken, bleeding mass. I closed my eyes, unable to bear it any longer, and when I opened them again, Dr. Mengerle had stopped hitting her. But instead of a human head, Ibi's tall, thin body carried a round, blood-red object, on its bony shoulders, an unrecognizable object, too horrible to look at. As he pushed her back into line and her long, emaciated legs took on the rhythm of the march, the bleeding head before my eyes turned into a globe, and it seemed to me as if Ibi's victimized body were carrying our war-torn, doomed Earth into the flames…And again I saw the little square, white house amidst the wheat fields, the teacher's house standing there as a symbol of freedom, brotherly love and of the striving for a better, more human world…

Half an hour later Dr. Mengerle returned to the hospital. He took a piece of perfumed soap out of his bag and whistling gaily, with a smile of deep satisfaction on his face, he began to wash his hands…

# THE BAG OF DIAMONDS

The month of August, 1944, covered the territory of Auschwitz with a heat wave never experienced before. The cruel Silesian sun was only one of the sources of heat, which, with a ruthlessness learned from the Nazis, burned deep wounds into our defenseless bodies. There was another source of heat somewhere outside the gates which sent a ripple of disquietude all through the camp. The crematories burned with a new fierceness and the passionate dance of the flames registered excitement, discontent with what was happening outside.

From morning till night we heard nothing but "Blocksperre," an order that meant curfew. The streets of the camp were empty, the doors of the blocks locked and we spent our days as well as our nights in the fetid darkness of the barracks. A prison within a prison.

We knew only too well what this "Blocksperre" meant. The thin walls could not keep out the whistling of the trains,—and trains to us meant new cattle cars filled with victims, new fuel for the never-resting crematories. Yet, there was something mysterious, something new and unexpected about this abundance of victims. We Hungarian Jews, who had spent many long months in this antechamber of death, could not quite understand it. We had believed that the Hungarian Jews were the last ones in Europe to be rounded up for extermination.

Some of the doctors, myself among them, were exempt from the curfew. In the transparent air of the August mornings we could see the columns marching from the train to the gates, well-dressed ladies, smart little boys and girls, each with his small bundle containing God-knows-what treasures. They marched, soundlessly, not knowing yet what was in store for them.

Suddenly I noticed a group of nuns in the colorful columns, their starched headdresses still immaculately clean. Blows and the coarse laughter of S.S. men accompanied their steps, but they seemed not to notice. Behind them I saw men in some kind of a uniform, maybe trainmen; behind them priests and then again elegant ladies with queer, big hats. Day after day they marched along the road, as if the Nazis had decided to exterminate Europe to the last man, woman and child.

One day I saw a group of well-dressed, white-bearded gentlemen go by, fully dressed, with hats and gloves and well-cut overcoats. They carried fine plaid blankets and small overnight cases in their hands, like diplomats going to some important conference...

I stood there, not far from the gas chambers, watching them, suffering for them, already mourning them. I saw their worried faces, questions in their eyes, but the answer, even if I had been able to communicate it to them, would have only added to their despair. One of the old gentlemen looked exactly like my father! Or was that only a fever-born illusion?

They were Dutch Jews, I heard, rich people, who had been able to hide until now thanks to their money and connections. But nothing could save them from the Nazis bent upon exterminating the last remaining Jews of Europe. They were all burned to death, quickly, before they had time to face their fate. Only a very few came out of the selection alive, dressed in rags like the rest of us.

A few days later I spoke to one of these newcomers. He worked on the refuse heap near the crematory. In that short time, the elegant, well-groomed man, who had looked like a diplomat, had become a dirty, lice-infected, human wreck, his spirits broken. He was a Dutchman and he spoke German.

I saw him go over to one of the camp foremen and whisper to him under his breath, anxiously, hurriedly. The foreman looked at him expectantly, and the new prisoner reached under his rags and brought out a small leather pouch, the kind which usually holds tobacco. He opened it with trembling hands and shook the contents into his palm. Like a million little suns the diamonds shone and sparkled in his dirty, broken-nailed hands. Grinning broadly the foreman nodded and held out three miserable uncooked potatoes, and the elderly man, shaking with impatience, tore them out of his hand and put them to his mouth, chewing, swallowing, as if every bite gave him a new lease on life. The little pouch full of diamonds already rested in the pocket of the foreman and he kept his hand on it, caressing the stones almost tenderly.

Here, in this Stock Exchange of Hell, the value of a bag of diamonds was three uncooked potatoes. And this value was the real one. Three potatoes had positive value, they prolonged life, gave strength to work and to withstand beatings, and strength meant life, even if for a short time only. The bag of diamonds itself was good for nothing. For a while, a short while, it might delight the eyes of a ruthless murderer, but when the day of reckoning came—it would not save his life ...

# THE LIFE-SAVING EMBRYO

The S.S. kitchen was one of the busiest places in camp. The cooking and baking went on for twelve hours a day, meal after meal was served, and the S.S. men and women grew fat on the rich food taken from the bundles of the newly arrived victims of the crematory.

Only Irma Greze refrained from overeating so as to keep her lovely body lithe and attractive for her future career as a movie star. She used to find a sadistic pleasure in putting all of my digestive glands to work by telling me about the meals she had and the ones she was going to have later. "We had real coffee with cream and sugar this morning," she would tell me, "and we ate Danish coffee cakes with raisins in them. The cook told me we are going to have roast loin of pork for dinner with browned potatoes and green vegetables." Her eyes never left my face while she spoke. There was a satisfied gleam in them as she noted the effect of her description.

A few old, "deserving" Aryan prisoners were the cooks in the S.S. kitchen, working under the supervision of an S.S. woman. The kitchen was the sanctum of the camp, heaven to the few prisoners who worked in it and a mythical place to those who only knew about it.

It was autumn—cold, wet and hopeless. We remembered, dimly, that there was a living world beyond the barbed wire fences, a world where people ate and drank and slept. Have they forgotten us? Have they forgotten this tremendous cemetery where only time separates the living from the dead?

It was night and I lay on the damp planks of my cot in the little "operating room" of our hospital, dreaming about the past, when suddenly I heard someone whisper in my ear: "Doctor—come with me—one of the kitchen superintendents wants to see you. You must examine her. Yes, I know, it is against the rules, but an order is an order. Come, I'll lead you..."

We stumbled through the thick mud covering the ground, surrounded by complete darkness. Suddenly I felt wonderful smells fill the air around me. Food, which a moment ago was but a dream, became a reality. My eyes filled with tears of intense desire and my usually dry mouth was wet with saliva.

We entered the lighted kitchen. Gleaming, well-scrubbed pots and pans stood on the racks along the walls. There were shelves full of fine china, plates, saucers, cups and dishes of various sizes. I breathed deeply of the rich smell of food which still lingered, hours after the last meal had been served. My eyes feasted on the sight of cleanliness and abundance which looked like something out of my own past. What would I have given to possess one of those cups, one of those silver spoons! Even the foul turnip soup we were given day after day would have tasted better had we eaten it out of a plate, with a silver spoon. But no use dreaming. These things were not for us—they were for our masters—the Nazis. My guide nudged me and we entered the room beyond the kitchen.

It was a lovely, young girl's room in white and pale-blue. Frilly curtains on the windows and a heavy, pale-blue silk spread on the bed. There were two comfortable arm-chairs and a writing desk. And in the middle of the room stood the S.S. woman who had sent for me, in a spotless white smock and high, black, patent-leather boots.

A short, crisp order: "Examine me. I think I am pregnant..."

I examined her and then straightened up. "I beg to report that there is no pregnancy present." And as a proof I held up my hand which was dripping with blood. For a moment her face softened. For a moment she was a woman, glad that her fears were groundless. "You can go," she said. "Tomorrow morning you'll get a pail of potatoes from me. But take good care that you don't blab..."

On our way out we again went through the kitchen and I could hardly refrain from touching the pans, the china, the glassware, the silver with a caressing hand. Then I was back on my cot to dream of potatoes for the rest of the night.

Before dawn somebody touched my shoulder. It was the same prisoner who had taken me to the kitchen super-intendent. In her hand she held a pail covered with rags, and in the pail there were about two pounds of potatoes. I dared not believe my eyes...The S.S. woman had kept her word. Potatoes—real potatoes...I took them in my hands, one by one, lifted them to my nose, my lips, to feel their fragrance, their texture... They were real. Not only a fig-ment of my excited imagination.

A second later I had wakened the entire medical staff, the four doctors and four nurses. Shifting my weight from one foot to the other with excitement, I told them about my treasure and how I had earned it. We were going to have a real dinner that night! We would get some water and boil the potatoes on the small iron stove of the hospital...Each of us had a different idea as to how to prepare them. One wanted to make paprika-potatoes, a favorite dish of many Hungarians...The other wanted to fry them in fat...A third dreamed of baking them in their jacket... It took a long time before we quieted down sufficiently to make a realistic plan. We would peel them with our surgical knives and boil them in water...

Never had the hours between dawn and dinner seemed as long as that day. Already a long line of sufferers stood in line before the hospital waiting for treatment, for bandages, for help. We hid the pail among the rags and went to work.

I shall always remember that day. I had been ordered to interrupt a two-month-old pregnancy and conserve the embryo in formaline. It was a difficult operation without instruments, without anesthetics, but Fate was merciful to me and I succeeded in bringing out the eight-week-old fetus in one piece. It was a beautiful specimen and I hurried to put it into the formaline jar to show it to Dr. Mengerle later. The mother, happy to be through with it, returned to work. Her life was safe—at least for a while...

My colleagues and I hardly spoke to each other in the rush of work, but when we did, our words concerned themselves exclusively with the potatoes. But we had to speak to our patients, as kind words were almost the only cure we had for their ailments. There were many broken bones to set, dog-bites to cleanse, whip-wounds to disinfect and skin afflictions to be treated with the small amount of salve we had. A few paper bandages and friendly words were all we could give these unfortunates. Yet, they liked to come. The hospital was the only place where they felt they could speak freely, remember their past, and make plans for their future. There was an illusion of security there, even though we all knew that disaster might bear down on us any minute.

Every afternoon, Dr. Mengerle paid the hospital a short visit. We feared these visits more than anything else, because he always found a reason to vent his sadistic fury on us and we never knew whether we would be permitted to continue to live after it.

Once we were abused because there were too many sick in the hospital, once because there were too few. Once he almost beat us because we were too dirty, another time he promised to have us cremated because we looked altogether too well-kept. He was free to do whatever he pleased with us—beat us, whip us, kick us with heavy boots or simply dispatch us to the crematory.

That day he was late. The afternoon was over, we had stood the second roll call, supper had been distributed, the stars were shining and still he did not appear. He had never been so late before—we told each other—maybe he wouldn't come at all. We began to breathe more freely and started preparations for our sumptuous evening meal. One of us left the hospital to fight for water, another went to gather little pieces of wood for our stove, a third walked down to the other end of the camp to beg a Polish woman, who worked in the kitchen, for some matches. I remained behind to sharpen our knives. A little while later we had everything we needed—water, wood, matches, knives...And all nine of us sat down on the grimy floor to peel our heavenly potatoes.

There was deep silence within the walls of the hospital, not a sound except our occasional low-voiced words and the gentle sound of the knife as it touched the juicy flesh of the potatoes.

Suddenly a car stopped before the entrance, the door was flung open, and before we had time to recover we saw Dr. Mengerle's dangerous, black-clad figure standing on the threshold. His mouth with the sharp, wolf's teeth remained open with surprise as he noticed what we were doing. We were completely paralyzed by fear and so were the two-hundred-eighty patients in the hospital behind us...

The silence lasted only a second, and the storm, when it broke, was all the more terrible. He ran around like a wild beast, smashing everything in his way. He kicked over the stove, stamped on our potatoes, overturned the operating table, screaming, shouting incessantly. "Yes...this is how I imagined a Jewish hospital. You dirty whores...You unspeakable Jew swine..."

I knew that this was the end. My poor potatoes, which I had shown my friends with so much pleasure, had brought death upon us and our two hundred eighty patients as well...I was sure that none of us would escape, that we were all condemned to death...

Suddenly I conceived a desperate plan. I got up from the floor, went to the shelf, took down the jar containing the fetus and approached Dr. Mengerle. *"Herr Hauptsturm-fuehrer* may be interested in this specimen..." I stammered. "Only rarely is it possible to bring it out in one piece..."

He stopped raving and grabbed the jar out of my hand. His face, which a moment before had looked like the face of a raving maniac, assumed a cruel, satisfied smile."Good...beautiful...Take it to Crematory No. II tomorrow. We are sending it to Berlin..." And as if he had forgotten what went on before, he turned around and left the hospital.

We calmed down our hysterical patients the best we could, and without a further glance at the squashed potatoes which almost caused our death, threw ourselves on our cots to dream of a world in which potatoes are a harmless vegetable for anyone to eat...

# THE STORY OF JEANETTE

Jeanette lived in Block 20 of the concentration camp at Auschwitz. This block which was like a stable was the so-called "maternity block," where Polish, Ukranian, Greek and Yugoslav women prisoners delivered their babies. There, too, the few Jewish women, who miraculously were still alive at the time the Nazi chief doctor's order extended the privilege of birth to them, delivered their babies.

Jeanette was French and a Parisian but she was very ugly. The city steeped in coquettish and harmonious beauty had obviously left no effect on her; she remained ugly. Her features were hard and masculine, and her quarrelsome personality was emphasized by the harsh sandpaper quality of her voice. She seemed to forget that she was surrounded by the constantly burning furnaces where death raged day and night, and she was unaware of the grotesque game being enacted in Block 20 by the perverse Nazi doctor. She considered her pregnancy as something very important and acted as though she were waiting to give birth in some private, elegant clinic in Paris. Each day was marked by new demands and increasing dissatisfaction; promises could hardly keep her comforted. No one liked her, no one understood her language, and the more she tried to impress her fellow-prisoners with her own extraordinary importance and that of her pregnancy, the more the others despised her.

But soon it was necessary to give Jeanette all the attention she craved—her labor-pains had started. She was not young any more. The tenseness of her abdomen and the intensity of her pains were not normal. In Auschwitz, delivery had to proceed quietly. Here any degree of suffering did not count, any body condition did not matter. But Jeanette's screams pervaded the camp: "Mon Dieu! Mon Dieu!" she cried, unmindful of her incongruous surroundings.

It was an abnormal birth—she gave birth to twins. We had to report this to the chief Nazi doctor. Dr. Mengerle was on the spot, in the cell ironically named "delivery-room." "Twins! Twins!" he shouted, and this magic word and all its implications reduced him to frantic, maniacal excitement. He paced back and forth in the narrow cell, and muttered repeatedly: "At last! The first twins are about to be born here!" And this sadist who seemed to have no other emotions at all, now completely lost his self-control.

Dr. Mengerle was not only the chief of the crematory but also its scientist. His hobby was twins. Skillful doctors did research under his order and control, to explain this secret of Nature: twins. His ambition was to multiply the *Herrenvolk* and to give to the German people the greatest manpower through twins. He performed the most execrable research on adult twins, and now he had the source of the secret—the newborn twins. He acted like a scientist who, after much tiring and exhausting research, had at last reached his goal and had discovered the heretofore hidden approach to the secret.

Ugly Jeanette became really important in Block 20, and Dr. Mengerle seemed to be very polite and thankful to the mother of the twins. He provided a basket for the twins; they received baby shirts; they were even given a blanket to cover their frail bodies. (In Auschwitz the newborn were clad only in dirty rags.) Jeanette lay alone on her stretcher, which even had a white sheet, and boasted of her achievement.

But the next day two sinister-looking S.S. men appeared in the block. "The twins, where are the twins?" they shouted, and took them away.

Jeanette fought like a lioness, talked incoherently and bemoaned her children. We tried to console her by saying that perhaps the twins were only to be examined, and that surely they would be returned. The entire maternity ward waited anxiously for the return of the twins. It was night when they were brought back. And thus from day to day, the French twins were taken away every morning and carried to a special laboratory where Dr. Mengerle performed his satanic research on them. During these hours Jeanette cried as only a mother can cry when her children are in great danger.

For fourteen days this torture of the mother's heart continued. And then one morning we found one of the twins dead—it had died, unable to endure life as a laboratory animal for Dr. Mengerle. A few days later, the other little Frenchman followed his brother—he couldn't endure the life of a guinea pig either. And Jeanette in vain filled the camp of Auschwitz with her cries: *"Mes enfants! Mes enfants!"*

Jeanette was no longer important. And when Dr. Mengerle appeared again and found that the twins had died, he became furious, and laughingly threw Jeanette into the crematory.

# LIQUIDATION OF CAMP C

The carefully planned campaign of exterminating all of Europe's Jewry included, among other things, death by overwork. While the Jews were in the camps, work was only a form of punishment, consisting of carrying stones or dirt from one pile to another and back again, but detachments of prisoners were constantly shipped off to Germany to slave in Nazi war industries. This practice of using Jews, of all people, to help their war effort must have caused much amusement to higher Nazi circles.

Every sixth month a large number of prisoners left for Germany in the preparation of the liquidation of the various camps. No camp was permitted to function longer than six months with the same set of prisoners. When the six months were over the camp was emptied to make room for the new contingent of victims. When the time for the liquidation of Camp C arrived, we knew what was awaiting us as we had already witnessed the liquidation of the Czechoslovak, the Gypsy and Russian camps.

There were thirty-two thousand Hungarian Jewish women in Camp C on that cold, rainy October day when our turn came. The process lasted for four weeks and at the end of those four weeks twenty thousand had been cre-

124

mated and twelve thousand sent to work in Germany. Only a few, among them we doctors, were placed in another camp to continue our miserable existence in Auschwitz.

At each morning's roll call Dr. Mengerle arrived, fresh, smiling, whistling an aria from Tosca or the Blue Danube waltz, which was one of his favorites. Behind him came a detachment of S.S. men armed with pistols and whips. They surrounded a couple of blocks and ordered the two to three thousand women to undress. Completely naked, these unhappy creatures were forced to run, between two rows of S.S. men who whipped them just for the fun of it, toward Dr. Mengerle, who looked them over one by one and decided whether they should live or die. Those who were too thin, those whose skin was covered with sores, those whose ankles were swollen and those whose bodies did not please him were sent "left." They were driven, naked as they were, out through the gates of the camp, straight into the furnaces.

The lucky ones, whose physiques were not yet completely ruined, were sent to the right. They were given a small bundle with a few pieces of bread in it and crowded into transports which carried them off to Germany to work for their worst enemies.

The nights we spent in the barrack during those four weeks were beyond imagination. Nobody slept, for we knew that every second brought us nearer to eternal sleep. Screams, complaints, prayers filled the air. Some fell prone to attacks of epilepsy and lay writhing on the floor with their mouths foaming. Some beat their heads hysterically against the wall. Some sat motionless, their eyes wide open, yet unconscious of what was going on around them.

We ran from block to block, trying to hide from our persecutors, but wherever we were they always found us and the only result of our effort was a terrific beating which left us weak and gasping. Who can ever forget those thousands of women who rushed around madly trying to find a loose brick, to break it into pieces and rub the red dust into their cheeks so as to seem strong and healthy when their turn came to face Dr. Mengerle? There was no escape. When the four weeks were over the barracks gaped empty into the autumn night, ready to receive another thirty-two thousand Jewish martyrs and house them for an infernal six months. The Hungarian Jewish women of Camp C had been taken care of.

# FAREWELL TO AUSCHWITZ

The first days of January 1945 were the coldest yet experienced in Auschwitz. Snow and ice covered the narrow streets between the barracks. Our feet froze to the ground during roll call, and those who had succeeded in retaining their health to a certain degree until now, came down with serious frostbites on their feet, hands, ears, noses. The warm tears of pain turned into shiny pearls of ice by the time they reached our cheeks and our lashes stood out stiff like so many tiny icicles.

At that time I was working in the Gypsy-camp, the former inmates of which had been exterminated. The ten to twelve empty barracks became the "sick-camp" of Auschwitz, filled to overflowing with incurable human wrecks lying in the warm, smelly steam emanating from feverish bodies and waiting quietly for death to come.

One of these barracks housed Dr. Mengerle's pets, the Polish and Hungarian Jewish midgets, about forty of them, some alone, some with their entire families. Their life was in many ways easier than ours. They did not have to stand roll call, they did not have to work, they were not beaten and their tiny bodies never fed the hungry furnace of the crematory. The healthy, the talented, the beautiful were ruthlessly exterminated, but everything abnormal was a source of constant amusement and enjoyment to our jailors because only when comparing themselves with these freaks could they feel superior.

There were days, though, when the midgets served other purposes than entertainment. Dr. Mengerle, the murderer, fancied himself in the role of a scientist and did a travesty of scientific research into the deficiencies which caused growth to stop in these little people. Often, altogether too often, he took great amounts of blood from their veins to play around with it in the laboratories reserved for German "scientists." The poor midgets grew paler and weaker as time went on, although Dr. Mengerle paid generously for the blood he took, by giving them a double ration of bread on such days. The ordinary bread ration, the same we received, was insufficient even for midgets. I shall never forget the little lady midget who told me one day that the double bread ration made her so happy that she did not even mind the cruel, painful and sickening process which made her earn it.

In another barrack Dr. Mengerle kept his other pets, the twins. To be a twin in Auschwitz seemed the maximum of good fortune. They were the chosen ones, the highest caste, the spoiled darlings of the S.S. doctor. They got the easiest jobs as superintendents of our various "institutions,"they did not have to appear at roll call, they received clothes, and shoes, and better food, their hair was not cut, and they were safe from being put to death in the usual fashion—by fire. It took some time before we found out that their fate was not so enviable, after all. Dr. Mengerle, who was so proud of his brute strength, of the power of his index finger which could distribute life or death at will, of his attractive, elegant physique, valued his sham-medical profession highest of all. The twins were only guinea pigs for him, well-fed guinea pigs in clean cages, but still just guinea pigs. Like the midgets, they too were subjected to continual blood-tests which left them exhausted and pale and full of fears of what was to come. Old prisoners, Aryans, kept the charts in the laboratories, the piles of notes grew on the tables and Dr. Mengerle went on with his feverish research to find out the causes of twin births.

The cold in camp grew worse and more unbearable. We wore the same clothes as in summer, received no blankets, and the lack of nourishing food weakened our resistance to the point where all we hoped and prayed for was death to deliver us from this torture. No human being has ever hated snow and ice with more concentrated violence than we did during that January. The rats, our only companions, became bolder and bolder; they snuggled close to our bodies at night as if they wanted to borrow some of our remaining warmth. Sometimes a sudden movement frightened them, and they sank their sharp teeth into our flesh, which resulted in more typhus cases, more festering sores, more death sentences.

I worked in Block 19, the barracks housing expectant mothers, women with hunger-edema whose swollen joints were filled with water, T.B. cases, women with heart disease and patients with serious frostbites—the incurables, the condemned.

Three of my best friends in this block were physicians. One of them had been a well-known oculist. Her husband had been a president of a bank, and she had two beautiful sons, who were put to death in Auschwitz. She had no ailment that could be diagnosed, but she was dying of exhaustion, hunger, thirst, cold, filth and the innumerable beatings she had received. For some incomprehensible reason she brought out the worst sadistic instincts in all the S.S. men and women and she was beaten more often and more cruelly than any of us. She had almost completely wasted away, nothing was alive about her any more except for two beautiful, wise eyes, which followed me around, full of affection and tenderness.

Anne, another physician, had tried to survive by simply ignoring everything that went on around her. For weeks after she arrived in Auschwitz, she had closed her eyes, her ears, and her mind to the horrors surrounding her. She had worked from morning till night, doggedly, unrelentingly, pretending that the world beyond the radius of her diligent hands did not exist. This went on until one day she came face to face with the furnace of the crematory and was given a piece of soap—soap made from the bodies of our parents and children. Then she collapsed. She stopped working, stopped eating, drinking, sleeping, but sat with her eyes open, motionless, soundless, mourning her six-year-old son whom she had brought here to die. One night she became feverish, then she contracted jaundice, and now she was lying there in Block 19, believing that I would cure her—with no other treatment than kind words.

Rose was a pediatrician—with the soul of a child. She had worked along-side of me from the first day of her arrival in Auschwitz. Her weapon against despair was optimism in the face of every hardship. She made up her mind that whatever our jailers did to us, they were powerless to destroy optimism and faith and wisdom. For eight long months, Rose was strong enough to keep up this pretense and fight every torture with faith, waiting for the Devil to run before the raised Crucifix. Then she, too, collapsed. Her wrists and ankles swelled, her heart knocked madly against her ribs and she began to gasp for air as if she were drowning. Her warm, child-like heart was broken by the inevitable loss of her faith and she was dying before my eyes without my being able to ease her suffering.

In another cage near Rose sat Betty, her legs drawn up under her like a Turk. Her checks were scarlet with fever and her ribs could be counted from a mile away, so far did they stand out of her emaciated body. She was young—nineteen years old—and after only eight months of imprisonment she was coughing up her lungs in pieces. Nothing meant anything to her any more, I represented the thin thread which tied her to life. I sat beside her as often and as long as I could, holding her thin, burning hand in mine and listening to her while she told me everything about her past life.

Her father had been a judge, a very cultured man with a deep love for music. He sent his daughter to the conservatory, while she was still a little girl, to study singing. Her teachers predicted a great future for Betty—success on all the concert stages of the world and due recognition for her lovely, powerful contralto...She had given two recitals before reaching the age of nineteen and both seemed to confirm her teachers' expectations. Then Betty fell in love. The young man was an excellent pianist and they had planned to marry and tour the world together. "You'll come to my wedding, won't you, Doctor?" she asked me repeatedly. "And you'll come to all our concerts...You'll sit in the first row and I'll sing for you alone...When I sing abroad I'll send an airplane for you, for you must always be there—always."

At night she sat on the edge of her bunk and, forgetting about her breathing difficulties, about the drops of blood appearing at the corner of her mouth, she sang one beautiful aria after another, Schubert, Grieg, Bach, Mozart. Her voice, still lovely and powerful, filled the entire barracks. The sick smothered their moans, the suffering forgot their pains, the freezing became oblivious to the cold. The reverent silence transformed the drafty, ugly, rat-infested barracks into a brilliant marble concert hall— the hideous faces looking down on her from the upper bunks were the powdered, rouged, smiling faces of the lucky few who occupied the boxes, and the ragged corpse-like creatures crouching on the cold floor of the block were elegant ladies in evening gowns and gentlemen in tails filling the red-plush chairs of the auditorium.

All the time she kept her burning eyes on my face as if I were the conductor, and she sang until a strong attack of coughing filled her poor tortured throat with blood. The minute she stopped, the world around us lost its ephemeral beauty and everything became ugliness, filth, despair...

Whenever I see the word "Six Million Dead" or "Six Million Jewish Victims" printed in a newspaper, my hands harden into fists and my heart beats stronger with revolt. Those six million dead are so many terrible, heartbreaking stories; they are Bettys and Roses and Annes, they are

Julikas and Charlotte Jungers, each and every one of them represents not only the second of death, however horrible that is, but an entire, colorful, exciting human life, a past, and what is more, a future…

In the bunk over Betty lay Ibi Hillman, daughter of a well-known and well-respected lumber man from my town. This girl, with her bronze-colored hair and peach-like complexion, her beautiful body and equally beautiful mind, was the pride of Maramaros Sziget. Wherever she went, people turned to watch her and happy were the few whom she called her friends. Yet, the inferno called Auschwitz engulfed her too. Her parents and entire family were sent "left" upon arrival, but the unusual beauty of the girl caught Dr. Mengerle's fancy.

She would have been better off had she perished with her parents in the flames of the crematory. A few days after her arrival, Dr. Mengerle picked her out of the lines at roll call. He ordered her to undress completely, feasted his eyes on her perfect body as yet unmarked by Auschwitz and sent her to Block 10.

There was an atmosphere of horror-filed mystery around Block 10. We knew it was the "Experiment Block" but none of us had any idea of what went on in there. This was where German "scientists" searched for the secrets of nature, using beautiful, young female bodies for vivisection. Only a few came back from there, most went directly to the crematory, and those who returned never spoke of what had happened to them. This is where young Ibi went. We never expected to see her again.

And then, one day, I received a message from her. She was in one of the "sick blocks" and wanted to see me. I hurried to visit her, but when I came face to face with her I didn't recognize her. The flower-like young girl was no more. In her place I saw a shrivelled, yellow-skinned little old woman, with hands and feet swollen to tremendous proportions. She had the marks of two major operations on her abdomen and her choking breath hardly permitted her to talk. She told me part of her story.

For six weeks she lived as though in a harem. She was well fed, well rested, kept meticulously clean. Then one day she was taken away, she knew not where, and she did not remember what happened to her afterwards. All she knew was that after a while she was thrown out into the camp, where she worked until she collapsed. Now she was here, looking up at me with tear-filled, trusting eyes, believing that I would cure her. I still don't know what they did to her when those insane perverts opened her up and I still do not understand why they permitted her to go on living after that experience. I tried to make her smile by bringing back memories from our life in Maramaros Sziget, by promising her that we would one day return to our beloved mountains and by providing her with little feminine thrills by stealing a piece of cloth, a comb, a few little luxury articles for her.

These were my closest friends, my most beloved patients in Block 19. But I loved others, too. I knew that even if I could not save them or cure them, my smiles, my tenderness, my promises of a better future helped them endure the last days of their lives. Their deep attachment to me, their need for affection, warmed my soul, and they in turn helped me to endure the innumerable sufferings of our daily life in Auschwitz.

Suddenly, towards the end of January, rumors started to run through camp life like wildfire. Auschwitz was being evacuated. Thousands and thousands of half-dead slaves were thrown into cattle cars and carted off, God knows where. The nights were loud with air raid alarms. Allied planes crossed the skies over our heads and the rumors became louder, more optimistic, more probable. The Russian counter-offensive had started.

The crematories were closing down. The Nazis were trying to hide the evidence of their bestiality. Auschwitz was going to be undermined and exploded. Everybody knew something, everybody had "reliable" information.

And indeed, transports left day after day and the number of inmates grew ever smaller. Yet, no one had a clear idea of what was happening. Then, one morning, fate reached out its hands to me. Dr. Mengerle sent for me. "Get ready. You are leaving Auschwitz!" he said. I stood there as if I had been struck by lightning. To go away, now, when freedom was so near? To go away when for the first time there was a hope for survival? To go and leave my patients behind to God knows what fate, the three doctors, and Ibi and Betty, who needed me, who depended on me? No! I could not go...

"You are still here?" Dr. Mengerle yelled at me. I tried to say something. It came out, stammering: "I cannot go away...I am sick...My eyes are infected..." It didn't help. "Get out of here!" was the answer.

I stumbled out of the office and went back to Block 19. As if in a dream I walked from bed to bed, smiling, laughing, not saying anything about the order. "The Russians are coming," I whispered in every ear, "hold out a little longer...The Russians are coming..."

I put my arms around every human wreck in the block, kissed the three doctors warmly, reminded Betty of her promise to send a plane for me when she was singing abroad and stroked the once beautiful Ibi's dry hair, repeating the pledge to walk with her in the snow-capped mountains behind our home-town. They believed my smiles, they believed my message of hope and not one of them felt the salty tears hiding behind my eyelids, ready to fall as soon as I turned my back to them. Then I left the block, spread a grey kerchief over my head, took my piece of black bread in my hand and went toward the gates of Auschwitz, where two armed S.S. men were waiting for me.

Some of the people who knew me saw me leave and came running to embrace me for the last time, but the guards were impatient. Blinded by tears, my heart full of the fear of the unknown, Prisoner 25,404 walked out of the gate...

This was not how I imagined it! During the interminable months, waiting for the day of liberation, I had seen myself again and again, leading my fellow-sufferers to freedom. I had seen myself walking ahead of them, laughing, crying, singing songs of freedom, a human being going to meet other human beings with gratitude and dignity, to thank them for our liberation...

Instead of this, I was walking over the snow and ice of the outskirts of the camp in my men's shoes of yellow leather, between two cruelly silent S.S. guards, into uncertainty, maybe into death...The barbed wire fence disappeared in the fog between us. The crematory did not function any longer and the sky was as grey and merciless as the ground under my feet.

What were they holding in store for me? How were they going to clear my memory of the acts of horror committed by them? How were they going to punish me for having saved lives they wanted to destroy? I relived every day spent in Auschwitz and was almost resigned to certain death when we arrived before a large wooden building. We must have been walking a long time, for the sun was almost down when we got there. Here is where I am going to die—I thought. I wish they would hurry and not make me suffer too long...

Suddenly I saw a German officer emerge from the building before me. I had never seen him before. He spoke to my guards, gave them a piece of paper and turned to me.

"You know too much...You are going away from here..." he sneered. "And look out that you don't try to run away...Or do anything equally foolish..." He lifted his heavy hand and struck me in the face. "Here is a little advance on what you are going to get!" he said.

I took the slap, standing up straight. I did not care what was to happen to me after this. My two guards saluted the officer, took me between them, and we set out on the icy road toward an unknown goal...

# TRIP TO HAMBURG

After the slap in the face administered to me by the Nazi officer I had no feeling, no thought left in my mind. I didn't care what was going to happen to me, I didn't care where we were going. I had no fight left, no fear, no revolt. The snow was like frozen wool under my thin shoes, soft and tiring to walk in, and emitting a cold dampness that seeped through the worn leather and turned my feet into numb, stumbling things which didn't feel as if they belonged to me at all. It was getting dark. Only the monotonous clap-clap made by the heavy boots of my guards broke the deadly silence of the foggy, unnatural landscape.

Out of the corners of my eyes I cast a secret glance at my jailers. One of them was a short, stocky, brown-haired man with a good-natured face. In his hand he carried an elegant pigskin briefcase. For a moment I thought of the man who must have owned that briefcase, of his wife who chose it for him with love and care, maybe a birthday present, and of the joyful celebration when he was presented with this delightful gift. I fought the impulse to stop my guard in his tracks and ask him: why? Why did he hate us so much, why did he use all his strength, all his ingenuity in devising new means of torturing us, innocent people

138

who were just like anyone else and who had never done him any harm. But what was the use? He wouldn't understand. He wouldn't even consider answering me except with a kick, for I, too, belonged to that helpless group of people whom they had decided to exterminate.

My other guard was a tall, blond fellow in a good uniform, with shiny boots. He must have had a higher rank than his companion. When he spoke to him, his words sounded like orders. He never looked at me, but walked on in silence with a cruel smile on his face which we prisoners had come to know as the Nazi smile. While the first guard was only cruel by profession, obeying orders when torturing us, this one looked cruel by predilection like someone who found his supreme fulfillment by seeing people, better than he, sink into moral degradation, inhuman suffering and, ultimately, death.

Suddenly, in the middle of nowhere, we stopped. My cold-faced guard walked a little way off to satisfy his urges. He stayed away quite a while and when left alone, the other one had the courage to address me. "Do you speak Roumanian?" he asked. "Yes." "I know that you were brought here from Transylvania," he continued, "that's where I come from, too."

"Are you going to kill me?" I asked quickly, urgently. "No...We are only taking you away from here—far away..."

The relief I felt was mixed with a strange bitterness. This man beside me, who had come to Auschwitz to take part in the annihilation of six million innocent people, came from Transylvania. He was one of the Swabians, the German minority of that country, a traitor to his homeland. Nazi by choice, not by any compulsion. I remembered the articles appearing in the Transylvanian newspapers: "Germans of Transylvania, unite! Join the great German Army!" He obeyed that call. He believed all the Nazi propaganda lies until, from an everyday person he had been turned into a murderous beast. Was he happier now?

The other guard returned and we continued on our way. It was completely dark by that time, only the phosphorescence of the snow guided our steps. To my surprise, I wasn't tired at all, although we had been steadily walking since early that morning. I thought of my patients in Block 19, who must have known by then that their doctor was gone...Maybe dead... And there would be no concert in the barracks that night...

It must have been around midnight when a few lights appeared in the distance. A village or a town—I thought with a joy which didn't last long. What good would a town do me? What could I expect from the inhabitants of a town under Nazi domination?

The lights became stronger and stronger and a little later we were walking through the deserted streets of a sleeping town. Only the heavy tread of German patrols proved that the place was inhabited. Then, suddenly we arrived at a tall, well-lighted building with a sign on it, reading: "Kattovice"...Yes, I remembered that station house! Our train had gone through it and I had stood by the narrow window, holding the hands of my husband and son, trying to decipher the name of the town. So here I was again, and still Prisoner No. 25,404...

My eyes, which for a long time had looked upon nothing but misery and death, the barbed wire fences of Auschwitz, the burning crematory and the trembling slaves dying

on their feet at roll call, were blinded by the strong lights
and the busy crowds of the station. Almost everybody was
in uniform, but there were a few civilians, too, talking excitedly, scurrying back and forth with their luggage, pushing, shouting for porters. This excitement was not the
usual atmosphere of railway stations. I felt that there was
more to it... These people were aware of some danger
coming... They were running away...

My two guards pushed me forward, keeping their
eyes on me as on some valuable piece of luggage. The station master looked through their papers, then we boarded
a train. It was a troop train, but in the third class we found a
place to sit down. I was dead tired and sleepy but not
enough to forget my fear. The soldiers around me all wore
S.S. uniforms. They didn't talk to each other, just smoked
in silence and sometimes reached for their haversacks to
cut off a big piece of bread and *Wurst*. The sight made my
mouth water and the dry crust of Auschwitz bread tasted
like sawdust...Gradually the men around me fell asleep,
except for my two guards who had to watch me. I looked
out of the window, wishing for death to put an end to
my suffering.

Then it was morning. The train ran through snowy
fields, on and on, through another day and another night.
My bones ached with tiredness, my stomach contracted
with hunger, the bread I had brought with me was gone
long ago. My guards took turns at sleeping and walking in
the corridors. Our only conversation consisted of my asking to go to the toilet, and even there they accompanied
me. I watched the young, determined faces of the S.S. lads

around me, trying to read their minds, trying to understand what had made them into the inhuman, unfeel-
ing, cruel beasts they were. But I couldn't understand
them...Could people that made Death their God be happy?
Did their conscience permit them to sleep at night, or did
they have no conscience at all?

None of them ever threw a glance in my direction. I
was a leper, a pariah, an untouchable. Hundreds of well-
fed soldiers and one sad, helpless, hungry woman...

It was morning again, the second morning since our
departure, and my hunger became stronger than my fear. I
took my courage in both hands, and turning to the guard
who came from Transylvania, begged him for some food.
Without a word he broke a piece off his loaf and pushed it
into my hands. That piece of bread brought warmth into
my blood and gave me enough strength to finish the journey without collapsing.

"Get ready, we are in Berlin," I was suddenly told later
in the day. Berlin! The city where I had spent so many of
my student years! The memory gave me new confidence.
We left the train and I breathed deeply the cold air of the
station. But my guards gave me no time to look around.
They pushed me into a completely empty, ice-cold room
without even a bench in it, locked the door and departed.
I was alone. I could break down and cry without shame,
without giving the Nazis satisfaction in my weakness.

I sat down with my back against the wall and
waited...Many hours later I heard the key turn in the lock
and my guards appeared, gay, red in the face, intoxicated
with beer. It was evening again. As we emerged into the

station I saw that there were more civilians than soldiers here. Married couples with children, carrying their own luggage, as there were not enough porters around, women, well-dressed, well-shod, with elegant fur coats and gloves, smelling of expensive perfumes, living on the riches of all Europe—and I among them, Prisoner No. 25,404, with my number displayed on the left breast of my ragged yellow coat…

People looked at me and turned away in disgust. Maybe they thought I was a convict, maybe a murderess— and all the time it was they who were the criminals, the thieves, the killers of women and children.

Again we sat in a train. It was morning, then noon, and about four o'clock in the afternoon we stopped at a station. Hamburg! I began to smile. Some time ago, to instill new courage in my patients, I had invented a war communiqué for them. I told them that Hamburg had fallen into the hands of the Allies, that American ships were sailing up the Elbe and that, with the fall of this northern stronghold, there was nothing to hold them up until they reached Berlin. There was a secret hope in my heart that my fairy tale coincided with the truth. But no! Hamburg was still in Nazi hands…

We got off the train—it was the fourth day of our trip —and we walked along the icy streets of Hamburg. I kept my eyes wide open to see the damage the war had brought on this city. Damage? There simply was no city left. Wherever I looked I saw ruins, lonely walls standing up like a warning finger, deep bomb craters in the places where houses had stood. Yet the remaining civilians were well-dressed, and occasionally a slow electric train rattled by, carrying people from their work to their homes. Destruction, ruin showed the way of the Allied planes, and yet I felt no elation. War is no solution to the problems of mankind. War has never yet led to permanent peace and security.

We walked on, endlessly...I was tortured by the cold and by hunger. People looked at me with horror in their eyes, and I looked back at them, as if to say: All of this is *your* fault! All this destruction and suffering and death. *You* started it! *You* are responsible for it!

The four days of our silent journey had made Auschwitz seem as unreal as our past life had seemed to us in Auschwitz. Only Block 19 was still close to my heart, Block 19 with its dying heroes who could still sing and listen to singing...

It was evening when we arrived before a large, grey factory building. Two elderly S.S. men guarded the entrance. We went through the gates and I still didn't know where we were. One of my guards asked for the Commander, who came out to meet us. He took the papers, looked at me and shouted for someone to come. A blond, cruel-faced S.S. woman appeared at his call and I was entrusted to her care. My two travelling companions, who had sat beside me for ninety-six hours without saying one word to me, took leave from the Commander and departed.

My new jailer shouted an order and I followed her, too tired to think. We ascended stairs, descended others, walked through long corridors and finally arrived in a yard cut off from the outside by a barbed wire fence. This is where they are going to kill me, I thought. But we went through a gate in the fence and I saw that we were in a camp like Auschwitz but smaller, surrounded by the same kind of electric wires. In the light cast by the fresh snow I could see rows of barracks in the background. My jailer took a key off a ring and opened one of the blocks. Frightened and curious eyes looked at me from the cots along the walls. The fetid, sickening smell told me where I was. A hospital again...But I had no strength to face anything that night. With my last reserve of strength I took off my yellow coat, put it on the cot under my head and collapsed. Fast, faster, as if I were falling, I fell into a deep, deathlike sleep.

# HAMBURG—DEGE-WERKE

Someone struck a gong outside, and a second later I heard the well-known call "roll call!" Still unspeakably weary, I got up from my cot, put on my ugly, yellow shoes and began to get acquainted with my new jail, my new jail-mates. It was still dark when we heard the keys of our S.S. guards turn in the lock. We were better guarded than in Auschwitz. There the electric wire fences would have foiled every attempt at flight; here there were heavy iron bars on the doors and their creaking signalled the beginning and the end of each day.

I learned that I was in one of Hamburg's suburbs, Wandsbeck, in the hospital of the *Dege-Werke*, a rubber industry serving the Nazi war effort. The camp was an *Arbeits-Lager*, a labor camp, for foreign slave workers and it was situated behind the factory buildings. The first roll call was at four o'clock in the morning and lasted one hour. At the end of that hour the day shift left for work under the supervision of S.S. woman guards. They worked hard for twelve hours, and when they returned there was a second roll call at five o'clock, after which the night shift left for twelve hours of work. Only the strong, the most enduring were ever brought to this camp. The work was hard,

146

exhausting, unhealthy; the foremen brutal and only too glad when they had an opportunity to use their whips.

One of the blocks was used as a hospital, under the care of a young Russian physician and a Polish and a Hungarian nurse. There was no crematory here, but there were two iron cages for those who showed resistance and in the middle of the camp the ever-ready gallows for those who tried to run away...

All this was whispered to me before the morning roll call, in German, Russian, Polish, Hungarian. While I was listening to these descriptions, I felt a terrible itching spread over my entire body. Lice! A new kind of lice, to the bites of which I was not yet accustomed...For breakfast we were given a cup of black coffee. The scalding liquid ran like fire through my blood and made the one hour roll call almost bearable. The smoking chimneys over my head were only factory chimneys—not the chimneys of the crematory furnaces burning the bodies of friends and relatives...

After roll call I was ordered to appear before the camp Commander. He was a short, stupid and brutal looking individual, and he talked like a drunken peasant.

"From now on you are responsible for the hospital. If you try to run away you'll be caught and hanged...And remember, I don't want too many patients in that hospital of yours...Those whores don't want to work; that's why they are playing sick all the time. I make you responsible for them and you'll be beaten if I find any malingerers in bed. There is work to be done here, you understand? Work! It is up to you to keep those whores from getting sick. Now get out of here!"

Now I knew what I had to expect. I returned to the hospital and began to work. The two months I spent in this work camp were heaven compared to Auschwitz. It was a prison, a hard and merciless prison, but the goal was work, not extermination. I regained my strength, which helped me to endure what was to come afterwards.

The hospital block housed about eighty to one hundred patients. There were cots along the walls, with thin straw sacks as mattresses and black, lice infested blankets. At one end of the block, there was a small room with a few water faucets. I even had some drugs, instruments, and bandages with which to treat the patients. The food was almost as bad as in Auschwitz, but there was more of it and we were given a piece of soap now and then.

At four in the morning I had to examine those who went to work on the day shift. During the day I treated the bedridden patients and at four in the afternoon I examined those who worked on the night shift. There was little time to sleep and I hardly ever had enough leisure to breathe some fresh air. The block was securely locked at five in the afternoon, after the departure of the night workers. I had a few typhoid cases, a great number of T.B. patients and the rest were industrial accidents.

I had been working for about two weeks, fighting disease and lice, trying to instill moral strength into my patients, when one morning I was accosted by a Russian prisoner who had news for me. "Doctor", she whispered, "Auschwitz has been liberated..."

For two days I went around in a red haze of pain, despair, fury. Auschwitz was free! Auschwitz has been liberated! I could be a free and happy human being today had they permitted me to stay there! I could have marched through those gates, as I had dreamed so often...I could have slapped the face of one of those beastly S.S. women! And here I was, a prisoner in Hamburg, helpless, still in deadly danger...Then after a while I calmed down again and, as before, gave all my thoughts to my sick fellow prisoners whom I had come to love like sisters.

I got to know Olga Singer, the Hungarian nurse at the hospital, the first day of my arrival. She had studied to become a mathematics and physics teacher and her father had been a famous rabbi. He, his wife and his other children were cremated in Auschwitz. Olga was the only Jew in our camp before I came, and as such the scape-goat of the guards and the S.S. personal. She had to do all the dirty work, carry bedpans, wash the sick, keep the hospital floor clean and scrub the blood off the operating table. In addition she was constantly beaten, kicked, abused, and received less food than the others. Yet, all the suffering she had to endure did not break her spirit. She was the best, the kindest, the most cheerful nurse anyone could wish for. No work, no sacrifice was too much for her. From morning till night she cleaned, washed, petted those human wrecks and often spent her nights at the bedside of a feverish patient, holding her hand and telling her gay, sweet stories which made the patient forget her pains. All of us adored Olga Singer. She was my only comfort, my only joy in this valley of tears. Her patience, her understanding, her never-waning concern for the fate of others gave me strength and a new will to live.

At night, when we had a little time to ourselves, she sat down on the edge of my cot and listened to my endless stories about my husband and my wonderful son, who were waiting for me somewhere and whom I wanted to be proud of me when we would again be free. I told her about our house and the sanitarium and begged her to come and live with us after all this was over. I was sure that both my husband and my son would love her and appreciate her extraordinary human values and charm.

Now, that the terrific tension, which in Auschwitz had kept me from thinking, was relaxed, I began to realize my losses. Only now did I have the leisure to mourn my wonderful parents, my brother, my sister-in-law. I did not know as yet that my only son, my pride and happiness, had also joined the number of those to be mourned...

Gradually I made Olga my assistant. I taught her how to make bandages, how to cleanse wounds, and showed her all the tricks of camp medicine. As her usefulness grew, the beating and abuses stopped. He physical strength returned and we found great happiness in being together. This friendship, originating in the Hamburg prison, accompanied me all through my terrible months in Belsen Bergen.

The physician who shared my work at Hamburg was a young Russian doctor, Marusa. She had come here from Leningrad and the hunger, the cold, the beatings and the exhaustion which had been her traveling companions caused an organic heart condition which made her almost too weak to work. We hid her condition—for which we had no medicaments—so as to keep her from being sent away. There were times when she was filled with a feverish optimism and sang gay songs of triumph and believed with the youthful ardor characteristic of Russians in the ultimate victory of her country. At other times she lay exhausted on her cot, mourning her eight-year-old daughter and her husband and yearning for the sight of her beloved Leningrad. And all the time, inexorably, her poor heart grew weaker and weaker…Then, one day she was taken away and we never found out what happened to her.

I believed then, and still believe, that talk was the greatest blessing, the only boon in those hopeless prison days. I saw women forget their pain, their fever, the beatings received and all physical suffering under the soothing effect of warm, friendly, understanding words. The past and the future were the only balm against the torture of the present.

The relative peace we enjoyed for a few weeks was soon over. Sometime in February 1945 air raid sirens shattered the silence of the night. Through the thin walls of our block we could hear the patter of running feet, then a command: "Everybody down on the floor! Roll yourselves in your blankets!"

Trembling with a new fear of annihilation, we lay on the damp floor waiting for the "All Clear" signal. We heard the humming of the approaching planes, followed the whistling of the bombs as they fell and, paralyzed, listened to the wild screams of terror and death. We were locked in, helpless, in a block only a few yards away from one of Germany's most important war factories. I was afraid. I had never been so afraid in my life. I wanted to live…I wanted to protect Olga, Marusa, my patients, myself. But all I could do was wait—wait…

From that day on the sirens went off and on all day, all night. Bombs fell incessantly on the town, which was already in ruins. We knew that every air raid, every bomb

that fell brought us nearer to freedom—if we only lived
long enough to enjoy it. We trembled with fear and expectation. We vacillated between hope and despair.

Hamburg was full of labor camps similar to ours and
the prisoners were used for cleaning up the rubble after
the air raids. As the shelters were not open to them, many
were killed, many severely wounded. Gradually my hospital became too small to shelter all these casualties and I was
given a second block filled with cots. The wounded were
brought in incessantly, with arms and legs torn off by
bombs, deep wounds in their heads, their ribs crushed by
falling bricks, some more dead than alive. All day long I
sewed, bandaged, put broken limbs in plaster and gave a
few moments of respite from pain to the dying...My ears
were filled with the shrieking of the sirens and the moans
of the bomb victims.

There was one cruelly cold night which stands out in
my memory. The air raid alarm had been on ever since
noon. Whoever had the strength to leave their cots lay on
the floor, rolled in blankets. We stuck pieces of rags into
our ears to keep out the sound of the anti-aircraft guns and
the eerie whistling of falling planes. Alternating waves of
hope and fear, flooded our souls and each of us turned to
our own God for salvation. The tension, the terror was
almost unbearable. Suddenly there was a noise outside, the
door was violently flung open and stretcher after stretcher
was brought with a woman in striped prisoner's garb on
each. Olga, Marusa and I hurried to receive thirty-eight
Czechoslovak, German and Jewish slaves, whose camp had
received a direct hit. Many had been killed, but some of the
wounded had been picked up and brought to us.

I worked in a desperate hurry for two days and two night to save the lives of these women. For two days and two nights I neither ate nor slept and had no other thought than the welfare of my patients. There were some who had their arms, legs and ribs broken, and by the time I was through with them they looked like mummies. One had lost both her eyes and I did not have the courage to tell her that she would never see again...For weeks I kept her eyes bandaged, promising her that when the bandage came off she would be able to see. There were two young women with damaged spines who lay on heir cots motionless, without a moan. And there were others, the lucky ones, who died after three or four days of suffering. Olga and I put their bodies into empty sacks and put them out behind the block.

My instruments were primitive, my medicines and bandages few; still, the help I gave was medical help. I made splints out of discarded pieces of wood and I am still proud of the limbs I nursed back to normal with the help of these splints. When, many months later, I returned to the hospital accompanied by a British officer, I found one of them on the ground. I picked it up and I still carry it around with me as proof of what ingenuity can do in the face of emergency.

Work and the fact that I was doing my professional duty helped me again to forget my own grief. I ceased to exist as a private individual. I knew that my work had an aim. Here I was a partisan, too, a partisan fighting against the Nazis by saving the lives they intended to destroy, by saving the future through keeping the young and strong women alive. I didn't feel the hardships of prison life any longer, but smiled and spread encouragement, faith, peace and the will to live...

My patients appreciated my care. One day, upon my entering the Czechoslovak corner of the hospital blocks, all of them began to sing a song written to me by one of them, a school teacher. This song was the greatest tribute a doctor could receive. I still carry a copy of it with me, and whenever I feel tired or discouraged I read its tender words, and warmed by its sincerity I feel again that a doctor's life is worth living under any circumstances. The poor young woman who wrote the words found her death on the rotting mountains of corpses in Belsen Bergen—after I had succeeded in saving her legs in Hamburg.

Day after day went by and I was waiting for the liberating armies who would open the doors of our camp and give us back our desperately hoped-for freedom. Those who worked in the factory, or outside, clearing away the ruins, brought rumor upon rumor, most of them exaggerated but all of them encouraging. "Breslau has fallen...Posen has fallen...The British are coming from the West...The Americans are approaching..." And at night, when our jailers locked the doors on us, we sat in the darkness and planned for the day of liberation.

On March 1, 1945, I received the most cruel beating of my entire camp life. It was in the afternoon, after an air-raid alarm, that one of the S.S. women came running into the hospital. "Where is the doctor? Inspection in a few minutes! Be ready!"

Feverishly I cleaned up the hospital, went from bed to bed to see whether my patients were in order, and already he was there—*Hauptsturmfuehrer* Weber, Commander of the camp, accompanied by a few S.S. officers. I stepped up before *Hauptsturmfuehrer* Weber, the dreaded "killer of Hamburg," and reported the number of patients, the number of doctors and nurses.

"Are you a Jew?" he asked me. "Yes." "Where did you came from?" From Auschwitz, *melde gehorsamst.*" "Los!" I could go. He walked through the two blocks, asked everybody what was wrong with them, until he suddenly stopped at the bedside of a young Russian woman who was lying in bed with incurable T.B., her cheeks burning under the heavy crown of blond hair. Her name was Katja and she was the sweetest, the most patient, meekest creature in the world. She kept a small rag in her bed for her bloody saliva, and she coughed the deadly bacilli into that rag. *Hauptsturmfuehrer* Weber noticed it, picked it up between his thick, begloved fingers and threw it into my face. "Is this what you learned in Auschwitz?" he shouted. "Auschwitz is supposed to be a good school for Jewish swine, I thought..." And, slapping my face with a violence that made one of my eye-teeth jump out of its socket, he walked out of the hospital.

My mouth bleeding profusely, I sat down on Katja's bed. My patients on the other cots began to cry piteously and those who could get up stood around me, caressing me, kissing my hands...Olga put her arms around my shoulder and I felt that we were all one body, one soul, and that none of us would ever forget, ever forgive this beating...

After the "inspection" I spent only a few more days in Hamburg. One morning, early, the camp commander arrived accompanied by a superintendent to make a list of all Jewish people in the camp. The list consisted of a number of patients, Olga and myself.

A little later a detachment of S.S. men came for us, to take us away, no one knew where. What were they going to do with those human wrecks, held together by bandages, wiring, plaster casts? What else but kill them? We had already heard rumors of the liquidation of all Hamburg camps. And what did liquidation mean in Nazi language if not death? The scenes I had experienced in Auschwitz repeated themselves in Hamburg. "Doctor Gisella... Stay with us... Don't let them take us away... What is going to happen to us?" they all cried in different languages.

A big black truck stopped in the middle of the camp and S.S. men were picking up the women, one by one, to throw them into it. I had to stand by, helpless, certain that this time we would not escape death. Now, when freedom was so near that we could feel its breeze on our cheeks, we had to die...Olga stood beside me on the truck. We were together. That was the only comfort left to us.

The truck roared through the burning city, then stopped at another camp where we spent the night. The next morning all who were able to move had to walk to the station, the others were carried on planks and thrown into cattle cars. A little later the long train with its load of frightened, hopeless Jews from all over Hamburg moved out of the station and was on its way towards an unknown destination...

# BELSEN BERGEN

The larger and smaller concentration camps throughout Germany were divided into two categories. The first category consisted of the work camps connected with German war industries, where the slave workers were mostly, but not always, Gentiles. The second category was the extermination camps, such as Auschwitz, Dachau, Grossrose, Dora, Buchenwald, Ravensbruck and a number of others, where organized murder was the only activity.

There was, however, a camp in northern Germany, between Hamburg and Hanover, which even the S.S. themselves designated as a "dung-heap". In Belsen Bergen there was not a sign of the famous German gift for organization. While in Auschwitz extermination was regulated by careful planning, here mass dying was consequence of lack of planning.

In January 1945, at the time of the big Russian counter-offensive, when Russian tanks were swiftly approaching to meet the British and American armies coming from the West and the South, Belsen Bergen became a dumping ground for prisoners evacuated from all other camps in Nazi-occupied territory. The highways were crowded with endless columns of marching slaves, almost naked in the icy winter, sick and starving human skeletons driven with whips and guns. Those who were too weak to keep up with the column were brained with gun butts. Dead bodies littered the ditches on both sides of the highway, indicating that other camps had previously been evacuated. Those who were brought to Belsen Bergen in cattle cars were no better off than those who had to walk. I passed many of those cars on my way to Belsen Bergen, saw the fleshless hands creeping out through the barred windows, heard the pitiful cries for bread—for water—for air—for death...Often these cars were put off on a side-rail and forgotten until they were destroyed when the Allies bombed the stations or until the stench of decomposing bodies reminded the Nazis of their existence...

The rope was tightening around the Nazis' necks and still, even in these hours of extreme emergency, they took time to drive these unfortunate helpless creatures toward the north, the nazi fortress, so that none of them should fall into Allied hands—alive...

Belsen Bergen was the terminal. It was supreme fulfillment of German sadism and bestiality. Belsen Bergen can never be described, because every language lacks the suitable words to depict its horrors. It cannot be imagined, because even the most pathological mind balks at such a picture. One must have seen those mountains of rotting corpses mixed with filth, with human excrement, where once in a while one noticed a slight movement caused by rats or by the death convulsion of a victim who had been thrown there alive. One must have smelled the unimaginable stench which lay over the camp like a thick cloud shutting out the air. One must have heard those unearthly screams of agony which continued through the day and the night, coming from hundreds of throats, unceasingly, unbearably...

In Belsen Bergen only a few blocks had cages along the walls. In the others, people were lying on the ground in their own filth—the living, the dying and the dead together. There were eighty to one hundred dead in each block, every day. There were no crematories to burn the bodies. They were left where they had died until someone who had enough strength left to move dragged them out and threw them on the dungheap. Everybody had typhus, everybody was covered with lice, eaten alive by rats, and there was no food, no water, no medicine. The narrow streets between the blocks were full of skeleton-like men and women who crept around in the dirt, searching for a drop of water, a bite of food, until, utterly exhausted, they sat down beside one of the mountains of corpses to die...Those who had enough vitality left to want to live on resorted to cannibalism. They opened the bodies of the recently dead and ate their liver, their hearts, their brains...

There was no roll call here, no selection, no work, no order. There was only death, a slow and horrible death from which there was no escape. New and new contingents of victims kept arriving, endlessly. At first they refused to believe their own eyes, tried to fight it, tried to survive. One could see them search the corpse mountains for their relatives, friends, acquaintances, breaking into wild sobs whenever they recognized the distorted face of a loved one. A little later they, themselves, were irrevocably lost in the inferno Belsen Bergen.

I arrived there on March 7, 1945, and the next day I

found the bodies of my brother and my twenty-year-old sister-in-law among the dead.

Nothing can prove Nazi bestiality better than the fact that even here our jailers, the ex-commander of Auschwitz and his henchmen, walked around clean, perfumed, well-fed, smiling. They had nothing to do; death did their work for them. Death held the whip, death called roll call, death prevented escape, revolt...The commander of this camp was a physician from Brasso, a Dr. Klein, who did everything in his power to prolong our suffering, make our death more horrible and ruin those who, by some miracle, could have saved their lives...

When the day of Liberation arrived, April 15, 1945, I saw British officers and soldiers weep at the sight which unfolded before their eyes. Even the most hardened warriors were crying, vomiting and cursing at this never-imagined depth of human depravity. When after their arrival we opened the warehouses, we found them filled to the brim with food, medicine, serums, bandages, that could have saved the lives of the entire camp had we only been permitted to use some of them.

Let no one speak to me of German culture, German civilization! Belsen Bergen was the faithful portrait of German civilization—Belsen Bergen mirrored the German soul...

# GENERAL GLEEN HUGHES

While in Auschwitz I believed that it was the site of ultimate horror, a place which made Dante's Inferno appear a musical comedy, and Hell, as described by the Catholic Church, a sinecure. When I arrived in Belsen Bergen I discovered that Auschwitz was no more than a Purgatory. Hell was enclosed between the barbed wire fences of Belsen Bergen.

In Auschwitz we still had the strength to keep our past alive and find comfort in re-living our memories. Here, as if our very brains had dried out, no thought came to our minds, our imagination refused to function; for had it dwelled on the sight which opened before our eyes, we would all have gone stark, raving mad. Our conversation was restricted to the essential topics: food—pain—death...

Surrounded by mountainous heaps of rotting corpses and by ditches full of bodies some of which still retained a breath of life but not the strength to climb out from under their dead companions, stood Block III, the "maternity block" of Belsen Bergen. From concentration camps all over Germany, pregnant women were sent here to bear their children in this torture chamber of Hell. There were German, Hungarian, Dutch, French, Gypsy, Russian, Polish, Czechoslovak women lying in the cages along the walls, two in each. Their tremendous stomachs, swollen to a bursting point with child and hunger, did not permit them to move, and their moans, their screams, their helpless cursing filled the building with a constant deafening cacophony. Lice covered their bodies in thick layers—hungry, persistent, insufferable lice sparing nobody, not even the faces and hands of the doctors.

Block III was my responsibility, but what can two empty hands do to relieve the indescribable suffering of hundreds?

Everybody in the block had typhus and, as if the disease were bent upon faithfully serving the Nazis, it came to Belsen Bergen in its most violent, most painful, deadliest form. The diarrhea caused by it became uncontrollable. It flooded the bottom of the cages, dripped through the cracks into the faces of the women lying in the cages below, and mixed with blood, pus and urine, formed a slimy, fetid mud on the floor of the barracks. Without water, without medicine, without help every attempt at life-saving seemed futile. And yet, the doctor in me never gave up even when the human being reached the limits of its endurance. I fought on with bare hands, cut my shirt into rags to wipe the hot, moist, soiled faces of my patients, tried to smile at them through the layer of filth that covered my own face and whispered hoarse, unconvincing words of comfort.

The air was so thick and humid that one could hardly breathe, the horrible smell of human excrement, blood, pus, and sweat invaded our nostrils in nauseating waves, until the desire for fresh air became just as torturing, just as unbearable as the desire for a mouthful of water, a bite of food. Our eyes hurt from the sight we couldn't escape, our eardrums hurt with the sounds we couldn't shut out. Burning compassion, helpless pity filled our souls until they, too, hurt like an open wound...

I had been working in Block III for several weeks, when around April 12, 1945, a whirlwind of excitement changed the atmosphere of the camp. Our S.S. guards left their posts and Hungarian soldiers with white armbands took over the policing of the camp. Something was happening beyond the barbed wire fences, something of great importance of which we were not told. And yet, rumors began to travel from mouth to mouth, wonderful, encouraging rumors, which for the moment seemed louder than the screams of those writhing in birth-pains. "The Allies are coming! The Liberators are coming!

Those who had the strength to get up came out of the barracks and went from group to group to listen to the news. "We are going to be free! We are going home! We can be human beings again! We can eat—drink—eat—drink..." Only the incorrigible pessimists did not believe in life: "They are going to kill us first," they moaned. Could the Nazis permit this proof of their bestiality to survive?

The camp was seething with joy, fear, uncertainty, hope, expectancy...

April 15, 1945. Young Marusa from Warsaw is about to bring her child into the world. In her superhuman pain she tears the filthy rags from her body, her dirty hair sticks wet to her pale forehead and she holds on, feverishly, to my dirty hands. "Help me, Doctor! Help me..."

Before having been brought to Belsen Bergen, Marusa was a member of the underground movement, the

Partisans in Warsaw. She had done everything a human being could do to fight the Nazis and then, eight months ago, she was caught and condemned to rot alive in Belsen Bergen. The child she carried under her heart grew on the hatred Marusa felt for the Nazis. It grew until April 15, 1945, when it was ready to leave the typhus-infected, lice-ridden, feverish body of its mother.

I did not leave her side even for a moment although the confused sounds coming from the outside came nearer and nearer. Suddenly I heard trumpets and immediately afterwards a tremendous shout of joy coming from thousands of throats shook the entire camp. The British have come! The Liberators have come! We are free...free.

Marusa's last scream of pain sounded almost jubilant...And a moment later there was between her legs the first free child born in Belsen Bergen. Pale and exhausted, the young mother could hardly smile, but the words leaving her bloodless lips were like a prayer: "Freedom...Freedom..."

The first free child of Belsen Bergen was safe. But her mother's blood wouldn't stop flowing. She grew paler, weaker and wide streams of blood came gushing out of her womb. My heart beat wildly. I had to save this Partisan mother! I had to save her! What did I care about freedom, about the British, about anything in the world if I couldn't save this heroic, tortured young mother! I ran out of the barrack and stopped the first British soldier I saw. Water! Get me water and a disinfectant! He didn't understand. I ran on and came face to face with a tall, impressive-looking soldier. With my bloody, dirty hands I grasped his sleeve. "Do you understand French?" he nodded. "Get me water

please, and some disinfectant...I have to perform an operation...Hurry...Hurry..."

He looked down on me from his tremendous height,
uncomprehending but moved to the core. He must be an
officer—I thought—a soldier who is used to the sight of
blood...And already I was pulling him by the sleeve, pulling him toward Block III. Half an hour later I had the
water, the disinfectant, and could wash my hands and perform the operation, not as a helpless prisoner, but as a doctor.

Here, in the first hour of liberty, I saved the lives of
the Partisan woman Marusa and of little Marusa, her
daughter. Many weeks later, when the young mother succeeded in overcoming the typhus, they both returned to
Warsaw to take part in the re-building of her beloved city.

The tall, hardened soldier looked on, with tears rolling down his cheeks. He could understand war, yes, and he
was not afraid of death. But what he saw in Belsen Bergen
was beyond the limit of his understanding, of his imagination. For weeks he fought, day and night, against sickness,
against death, against lice, against starvation. He did
much, but in most cases he was too late. Yet, he was a real
liberator. All the inmates of Belsen Bergen who survived
will forever bless his name. He was Brigadier General
Gleen Hughes, head of the Second British Army.

# ABBÉ BRAND

April, 1945. A long line of British tanks and jeeps came rolling into the death camp of Belsen Bergen. The dead were all there to receive them, lying along the road, in the ditches and on top of the mountains of decaying, putrid corpses; but only a few of the survivors had strength enough to crawl out of their holes and salute the victors.

Rivers of blood, pus and human excrement flowed lazily across the road and the fetid steam rising from them covered the camp like a heavy, smothering cloud. The strange, terrifying beings who were once men and women, before hunger and disease stripped them of their human appearance, slowed down the progress of the saviors, because they lacked the strength to get out of the way of the tanks.

Without any waste of time, the British went to work. They provided food for the bloated stomachs, established field hospitals by the hundreds, fought against rats and lice and tried to create an atmosphere in which the re-birth of the desire to live was possible. In the cases of many they were too late. In spite of their relentless work, the liberated inmates died by the hundreds and new mass graves had to be dug to receive their tortured, disease-ridden bodies.

It was June when Abbé Brand arrived in Belsen Bergen. His fame spread like wildfire through the camp. There is a young priest here—people said to each other— who comforts the suffering, feeds the hungry and holds the hands of the dying with so much love and compassion that his mere touch eases the pain and banishes the fear of death. He never asks others about their religion and does not care in which language they speak to their God.

At that time, I was working at the gynecological-surgical hospital R-5, where young mothers, girls, children and babies fought for life which now was identical with freedom. I shall never forget him as I saw him that first day, with his black cape over a British army uniform, his big silver cross on a chain around his neck, his dark, burning eyes, and his young face showing the signs of intense suffering.

"I am Abbé Brand," he said to me in French, "and I am a member of the Vatican Mission. If there is anything I can do for you, help you in your work, help you ease the pain of your patients, please accept my helping hand..."

There was such warmth, such real Christian love in his simple words, that the answer stuck in my throat and only my tears expressed the deep gratitude I felt for this man of God. I showed him around the hospital, and while we walked words kept stumbling out of my mouth. I told him about Auschwitz, about the pregnant mothers and newborn babies who had to die in the flames, about my tragic efforts to save their lives and about the inhuman suffering it cost me to prevent birth, the greatest, most beautiful miracle in the world.

I spoke about my patients in Belsen Bergen, where it

was again permitted to give birth, where sick mothers, suffering from typhus, starvation, exhaustion, revived at the
sight of their newborn babies and gained new strength
from the knowledge that their children needed them. I
told him about my happiness when I awoke to the sound of
babies crying and went to sleep at night with the wailing of
those tiny human beings still ringing in my ears. "And I
have no sugar," I said, "no milk, no rice to feed these wasted
bodies. They need more nourishment, more wholesome
food if they are to be saved..." He never interrupted me,
only his young head bent deeper and deeper as if the
weight of sorrow and pain were too heavy to bear.

The next day a truck stopped before the hospital, a
truck filled with all the things we needed, sugar milk, rice,
chocolate in large quantities. The little priest, that's what
every one called him in camp, unloaded the truck himself.
He carried the heavy sacks and cartons until our little
stockroom was filled with food, and then he went from bed
to bed handing a piece of chocolate to everybody, with a
smile that was even sweeter than the delicacy he distributed.

From then on the little priest was a frequent visitor at
the hospital. His hands were soft on the foreheads of the
dying, cool and strong when they held down the body of a
patient who fought against nightmares in her feverish
dreams. His magic eyes brought love and comfort to everyone, French Catholics, Dutch Protestants, Hungarian Jews,
or adherents of the Russian Orthodox faith.

Sometimes he appeared early in the morning or late
at night, his face damp with exhaustion, to tell me about
some one dying in Block 39, a man screaming with pain in

Block 51, a woman collapsing in the street. "Maybe you can help, Doctor" he said, "at least come and take a look at them.." And already he dragged me by the hand, telling me to hurry, to hurry before it was too late. Day after day I watched him getting thinner, more ethereal, more transparent. He was never hungry, he was never tired, because there were always others who were hungrier than he, more tired than he. Only his eyes grew larger in his pale face, larger, more luminous and burning with the fever to help.

It was in the middle of the summer of 1945. We knew that in the gardens of the world fruit was ripening, vegetables were growing, but it was not for us. The barbed wire fences still stood around Belsen Bergen, and beyond the fences there was nothing but dry, empty flatness and beyond the German villages, inaccessible to the inmates of the camp.

Abbé Brand knew our needs as he knew our thoughts and dreams. One morning he left the camp to visit the farms around us and in the evening he returned with vegetables, lettuce, apples to enrich our table with the sorely needed and badly missed vitamins. He was happy to give, happy as a mother when she feeds her child.

Later he brought toys for the children, dolls and toy animals, books full of fairy tales and beautiful pictures. There was nothing he would not do to make our lives real, enjoyable and worth living.

He always knew where he was needed and it did not matter to him whether it was day or night, rain or sunshine if any one yearned for the comfort of his presence. Sometimes we did not see him for a week; then we knew that he had left for another camp to carry his love, his kindness, his helpfulness to the victims of Nazi inhumanity. When he returned, he would be thinner, sadder, his white hands more transparent, only the cross on his breast seemed to grow and become more shiny all the time.

His truck was never empty when he returned. Sometimes he brought a sick man or woman to our hospital, hoping that our care would still be able to save them; sometimes he brought a mother whose child he knew in Belsen Bergen, a sister or brother or child whose relative, he knew, was still alive in our camp.

When someone needed a dress, they asked the little priest. Shoes, paper, warm clothing—he never said it was impossible and nothing seemed to be impossible for him. He gave and gave, smiling, with infinite love as if giving were the only aim, the only dream of his life.

One day I decided to prepare a surprise which would make Abbé Brand happy. We were great friends and it meant much to me to be able to do something for him. I emptied one room of my hospital, put a table at the end and, facing the table I put as many chairs as I could get. Then I walked all over the camp, collecting flowers, which I put in that room. By Sunday Abbé Brand had a church in which to celebrate Mass, his first Mass in Belsen Bergen.

Who can ever forget the happiness in his eyes when he entered the room and saw all the patients who were able to get out of bed sitting there, some with their babies in their arms. They were all there, Catholic and Protestant and Jew and Greek Orthodox, and Abbé Brand spoke to them in German—about Love...

In the afternoon he came back to baptize the first children born in Belsen Bergen. After this he celebrated

Mass every Sunday morning, until one day, many weeks
late, he was called to Paris. How empty the camp seemed
without him. How cold and sad it suddenly became. Wherever I went I heard the sick and the healthy speak about
him, about our little priest, wondering when he would
return.

Suddenly he was back again, his hands full of
presents, food for the adults, toys and books for the children. He asked me and the nurses to come into the office
and there he handed each of us a little parcel. "I brought
this for you from the Galeries LaFayettes," he said, "I hope
you'll like it. I don't understand about these things, I am a
priest, but I wanted you to be women again, not only
workers, and I want you to enjoy your youth..."

There was some face powder in that parcel, a piece of
soap and a little perfume. A message from Paris, a message
from the big, free world...He wanted us to forget Belsen
Bergen for a moment, to forget the blood, the filth, the
endless agony and our own helplessness in the face of
death.

"Love" was cheap in Belsen Bergen. The liberated
thousands, completely demoralized by long years of Nazi
oppression, had no other aim than to satisfy their most
basic instincts, hunger and sexual desire.

Some sought "love" because it made them feel like
human beings again; others because they wanted to prove
to themselves that they were still men and women; others
again because they wanted to enjoy their newly won freedom to the fullest. Then, there were some who sold their
bodies for cigarettes, chocolate and other small comforts.

Abbé Brand watched this open prostitution, which he

did not know how to stop, with ever-growing despair. The authorities could not help him, for they were not inclined to use drastic means aginst these people who had suffered hell. Abbé Brand set out alone. Wherever he went he saw couples locked in an embrace, on benches, leaning against trees, at deserted corners...Sometimes the man wore the uniform of the British army, sometimes it was one of the prisoners who only a few weeks ago believed that his life was finished. He stopped the men and women and began talking to them. First he asked them to tell him the story of their lives, in every detail, until the past surrounded them like a veil shutting out the present. Then, only then, he spoke to them about the future.

"You are free now..." he told them, "free like newborn children with the paths of life open before you. Why don't you try to start this new life free and unencumbered? I understand your drives and desires, but remember, you have many difficulties to face and you will need all your physical and moral strength. Pregnancy and venereal diseases will make your task only more difficult and complicated."

To those who were willing to listen, he depicted the future, a fighting future which was worth any effort and self-denial. His pockets were always full of cigarettes and chocolate and many a time he prevented prostitution by giving generously and freely. Sometimes he was laughed at, mocked, abused, but he never gave up, and the results of his relentless work could soon be felt toughout the entire camp.

In Room No. 12 there was a dead girl on the bed. Her mother, a young woman of 38, lay in the other bed beside her daughter. She had typhus but it was not only the fever that racked her thin, wasted body. In her delirium she spoke constantly about her daughter, Agnes, about the past, the present and the future—but always in connection with her daughter. For two years this woman had protected her sixteen-year old daughter; they had been at Auschwitz, then in a war factory near Hamburg and finally in Belsen Bergen. She had given her bread, her soup to the child; she had held her close to protect her against the cold, against blows and brutality; and now, when they were finally free, Agnes died—left her forever.

Abbé Brand sat by her bed for hours at a time. He knew, as we knew, that her case was hopeless. For hours he listened to the screams, the curses, the sacrilegious words of the unfortunate mother, never blaming her, never losing his patience.

One morning she sat up in bed and kept her eyes on the door until Abbé Brand entered the room. Then she began to scream. "I want a tomb stone for my Agnes, Abbé, I want a memorial for her. I won't get out of here until I have the tomb stone for my daughter…"

The little priest laid her gently back on her pillow. "I have thought of it myself," he said, "Agnes must have a tomb stone and she shall have it—but you must be patient."

We smiled sadly. A tomb stone in Belsen Bergen, where the mass graves were never big enough, never deep enough to receive the dead, where the British army toiled like saves to satisfy primary necessities of the camp. But the Abbé had promised. And he had never broken a promise before.

Many days went by. Agnes' mother got better and better. The priest came to see her every day and they sat on the edge of her bed, their heads close together, whispering excitedly as if they had a great secret together. Then, when the poor mother was strong enough to stand on her feet, Abbé Brand came to speak to me.

"Doctor," he said, "tomorrow I want you to come with me, we are going to Agnes' grave."

The next morning the entire hospital waited excitedly for the arrival of the priest. When we finally saw him coming down the road, he looked like a young Moses with the stone tablets in his hands. He carried a grave marker—made of wood, beautifully worked, with big blue letters on it, saying: "Here lies our Agnes, to remain with us forever."

He put the tablet into the hands of the mother, who looked at it with tears in her eyes, tears of gratitude and solace.

Then we set out toward the grave. Abbé Brand went ahead holding Agnes' mother by the arm—the Jewish woman, the Catholic priest. Behind them came people of many nationalities and many religions, united by common suffering, loyalty and love. At the grave, Abbé Brand knelt down on the ground and put the hand-made monument into the soft earth. Then he got up and began to pray, "In nomine Dei..."

When he finished his prayer he turned to the mother. "Agnes is happy now...She looks down upon her mother and many friends and sends them peace... Amen..."

Then he led her back to her bed at the hospital, cured in body and in soul. I don't know whether that little tomb stone still stands in Belsen Bergen, but I hope it is there, in memory of a dead child, and in memory of a great heart, Abbé Brand, who will never cease, as long as he lives, to give peace and kindness to those who need it...

It was Fall. There were fewer and fewer people in the camp. The French, Dutch, Czechoslovaks, Yugoslavs who survived typhus and T.B. returned to their countries. But there were still thousands left behind, the sick and the homeless Jews. They had no place to go, nobody was waiting for them, no country wanted to have them back. Disillusioned, hopeless, they lived from day to day.

Yom Kippur, the Day of Atonement, was coming, the first free Yom Kippur in Belsen Bergen, without parents, without children, without families. My hospital was full; it had a good name and women from many camps came to seek a cure for their ills.

Before the holiday I spoke to our little priest. I wanted to have my patients celebrate their holiday, with many candles and a feast table, in honor of our dead...He, the twenty-six-year old wise, kind priest, understood. He brought candles, honey, fruit and many cans of food, and a bunch of flowers for every patient who was unable to leave her bed.

When, the next day, I got up to speak at our table, I spoke to him, Abbé Brand, who made it possible for us to celebrate our Jewish holiday, who made it possible for us to live.

A few weeks later Abbé Brand played a very important role in my life. The American Joint Distribution Committee in Paris informed the Belsen Bergen authorities that I had received a priority certificate for Palestine. I left Belsen Bergen to wander from one camp to the other throughout Germany, trying to find my husband, my son. After nineteen days of wandering on foot, along destroyed highways, I learned that my husband had been beaten to death shortly before the liberation and my son had been cremated...

When I returned to Belsen Bergen I did not want to live. There was enough poison at the hospital, poison which in small quantities served as medicine. I took some of it. Later I learned that Abbé Brand, who had been away for weeks chose that particular day to return to Belsen Bergen. He came to my room and found me lying on my bed. He ran for the British physician, who was just in time to save my life. When I came to, I saw Abbé Brand sitting by my bed, holding his big silver cross, praying. He came to see me several times a day. He had a telephone installed in my room and when he couldn't come he telephoned, to give me courage, to share with me his faith, to give me a new will to live. He was my doctor, my friend, my savior and I understood, better than ever, why the sick and dying loved him so much.

When I was strong enough to get up, I returned to my work, half insane with pain and sorrow, like a wounded animal. In the meantime, Abbé Brand obtained papers, permits, corresponded with Paris, and one autumn morning the white car of the Vatican Mission stopped in front of the hospital. There was an armchair in it for me. And a little later the car rolled through the gates of Belsen Bergen, leaving behind the barbed wire fence and all it represented.

We travelled for two and a half days. At night he made me rest, first at a Dutch, then at a Belgian convent, and during the day he treated me like sick child. The third day we arrived in Paris. My eyes hurt from the many lights, my ears from the noise. What was to happen to me? Where was I to go?

Abbé Brand stopped the truck and led me into a beautiful, elegant home. It was the home of a French dentist, in one of the residential sections of Paris. "I brought you a wonderful woman from Belsen Bergen," the little priest told them, "a woman whose soul is still very ill after all the horrors of many prison camps. Take care of her until tomorrow morning. I shall sleep in the truck with the driver. Sleep well," he said to me, "you are safe here in the house of my old friends." He reached under his black cape and brought out a bottle of good old wine. "I want you to celebrate your first evening in Paris."

That evening was like a dream. Good food, wine, interesting conversation, wonderful French manners. We spoke about Abbé Brand. My hosts, too, loved him and considered him a saint. Afterwards I slept in a real bed, between silken sheets.

In the morning he came to get me. I was to stay at a convent in the Rue de la Tombe Issoire, and he asked the Mother Superior to take good care of me. But he did not leave me yet. He went with me to the Joint Distribution Committee and the Palestine Bureau, and fought for me, for my future, as if he, the Catholic priest, carried the tragedy of the entire Jewish people on his shoulders.

Then he returned to Belsen Bergen and I remained at the convent trying to regain my health, my balance. The Abbé wrote me encouraging letters and slowly, very slowly, I began to feel human again. A few weeks later he came back to Paris, thinner, paler than I remembered him. His mission at Belsen Bergen was finished and he was going away. Before he left he kissed my forehead and looked sadly at the concentration camp number on my arm. He asked me to believe in love and to give love wherever I go. Then he disappeared into the cold, rainy autumn night...